WHY REAGANOMICS AND KEYNESIAN ECONOMICS FAILED

Why Reaganomics and Keynesian Economics Failed

James E. Sawyer
Associate Professor of Public Service
Seattle University

St. Martin's Press   New York

First published in the United States of America in 1987

Printed in Hong Kong

ISBN 0-312-00532-6

Library of Congress Cataloging-in-Publication Data
Sawyer, James E., 1943–
Why Reaganomics and Keynesian economics failed.
Bibliography: p.
Includes index.
1. United States—Economic policy—1981–   .
2. United States—Economic conditions—1981–   .
3. Supply-side economics—United States.   4 Keynesian
economics.   I. Title.
HC106.8.S28   1987   338.973   87–9578
ISBN 0-312-00532-6

For Gail; and in memory of my parents

Contents

List of Tables

List of Figures

Part I

The Issues

America is becoming a stationary society with little economic growth, and therefore little opportunity for economic mobility. Productivity improvement is the crucial component of economic growth – and productivity has been moribund for the better part of two decades. Many proposals have been advanced to cope with declining productivity. Reaganomics is one of them, and it has been revealed as a failure.

The roots of American productivity decline are far deeper and more onerous than most Americans recognize. At the very heart of the matter lie theoretical problems which cause households and businesses to pursue self-interested action which may be damaging to the interests of society. Certain financial practices – such as corporate raids – may be justified by the theory taught in business schools, but they may also be deleterious to aggregate economic well-being. Only a correction of economic policy – and the correction of the economic theory which empowers it – can resolve the productivity problem which is the greatest threat to economic progress in the concluding years of this century.

1 Introduction

If the American dream is not dead, then surely it is in intensive care. Consider this. Compensation per hour, adjusted for inflation, grew at a compound rate of about 3 per cent in the twenty-year period between 1948 and 1968. This meant that the family of a typical worker could consume about 3 per cent more each year, year after year. At that rate the standard of living was doubling about once every generation. But a dramatic change took place in the American economy between 1968 and 1973, approximately contiguous with the Vietnam War. In the twelve-year period since 1973, real hourly compensation increased at a rate of about three-tenths of 1 per cent per year. This means that the standard of living of the typical American family is doubling only at a rate of about once every few hundred years!

Americans have become confused about the economic problem. During the 1970s it was thought to be inflation, while in the early part of this decade it was thought to be high interest rates. But these have been delusions that have masked the real problem, which is economic growth. Our society, as Lester Thurow describes it, has become a zero-sum society. The only way someone can become better off economically, in general, is for someone else simultaneously to become worse off.

In many ways, 1973 was the last good year. Since then growth has largely stopped and wages and incomes have shown the effects of stagnation. For instance, consider the expectations of a typical young American male passing from age 25 to age 35. During the 1950s or 1960s, his earnings would have more than doubled, adjusted for inflation. But for the typical male making the transition after 1973, earnings grew by only 16 per cent – a fraction of what was expected a few years before. The outcome has become even more bleak for middle-aged males. A man passing from 40 to 50 prior to 1973 could have expected his earnings to grow by 30 per cent. After 1973, however, a comparable individual actually experienced a 14 per cent decline in inflation-adjusted earnings.

People in their 20s, today, grew up with the television family of Howard and Marian Cunningham, their two children, and various family friends. We glimpsed 'The Great American Dream' as it might be for ourselves, if we worked hard, got a good education like Richie

3

did, and maybe went into business as Mr C. did. Included in the
scenario were a beautiful home and a new car every once in awhile.
Mrs C. was always at home making pot roast, baking cookies, and
generally lending high support to the Cunningham clan.

But no more. The 1980s have been dubbed the decade of 'cutback
management'. It has rendered the Cunninghams' dream remote, if
not impossible for most Americans. We live in an era in which less
expense is better than more revenue. It is a decade of white-collar
unemployment, mounting poverty, and the decimation of former
industrial giants such as steel. It is a decade of 'running lean and
mean'. To compete effectively, we must accomplish more, we must
do it better, and we must do it with fewer people. In our organizations there is precious little time to think, but only time to act, to
react; barely enough time to keep ahead of – or perhaps only even
with – the competition. Rush here, rush there, do more, excel! But
with all our doing, economic society does not grow larger or better. It
simply becomes rearranged like coloured pieces of a kaleidoscope.
No matter how the pieces may be assembled, studied and refracted,
they constitute only a stationary quantity.

LAYING THE BLAME

Upon whom do we pin the blame for this economic mess? Is it
Lyndon Johnson, Jimmy Carter and the liberal 'Keynesian Demo-
crat' presidents of the 1960s and 1970s? Or is it Ronald Reagan and
the 'supply-side' conservatives of the 1980s? Actually, responsibility
rests with both, for neither side possesses the 'holy grail'. Slow
growth and inflation certainly plagued Americans during the 1970s
because of Keynesian policies. Ronald Reagan was elected in 1980 on
a mandate to get the country moving again, economically. But the
economy has continued to move in the wrong direction under his
stewardship, and at a perilous price.

Reaganomics alleged that a tax cut to the rich would encourage
saving and investment, and therefore growth. In 1981, Congress
reduced tax revenues by approximately $125 billion per year on the
assumption that economic growth would create a tax base sufficient
to replenish lost revenues. But the assumptions of Reaganomics were
unrealistic, if not farcical. Between 1981 and 1985 the national debt
soared from 1 to 2 trillion dollars. Two-thirds of this second trillion
dollars in red ink can be traced directly to the tax cut. A haemor-

rhaging of losses from international trade also propelled the United States to the status of a net debtor nation in 1985, for the first time since the First World War.

America is becoming a poorer nation and the ideologues are not without their responsibilities for the failure. Neither side has the truth. It is the reality of our time that the standard solutions of the political right or the political left cannot solve our problems. Even the nature of our problems has changed, so that we may not recognize them and take some action to avert further deleterious consequences. Indeed, we live in a time in which the paradigms upon which our economic wisdom is built have been brought to crisis.

Lots of excuses for failure are given by the defenders of both the conservative and the liberal versions of the 'conventional wisdom'. The excuses include blaming the workers, or blaming the managers, or simply disavowing that a problem exists. Simplistic solutions no longer work, nor do they even make sense. We must start afresh, by examining the very roots of economic thought. In so doing we shall find significant connections between our economic failures and the intellectual apparatus used by economists for 200 years to explain and to predict economic behaviour.

NATURAL LAW

Economics claims to be a science but its foundations go back at least 200 years to the study of moral philosophy, which had its basis in natural law. Natural law is a study of the fundamental principles that order the universe. It hypothesizes that a perfect order may exist, and that human happiness depends upon living in harmony with the laws of that order. It is significant to recognize that the foundation of economic science is not based upon verifiable observation, but upon an eighteenth-century metaphysical system. Even so, economists continue to use that system as if it is value-free, when it implicitly conveys profound judgements of value. It is the contemporary inappropriateness of some of these value judgements made 200 years ago that renders the theory unable to explain and to predict. Our goal should not be to dismiss 200 years of economic thought. Rather, it should be to correct the intellectual system so that it portrays the contemporary economic tableau realistically.

LAISSEZ-FAIRE

Literally interpreted, *laissez-faire* means to let it be or to let it go.
During the eighteenth century it was a doctrinaire prescription for
the organization of society. In an era of strengthening nation states,
laissez-faire argued that the happiness of citizens would be enhanced
through the minimization of government intervention. With regard
to the economy, the doctrine argued that the pursuit of personal
greed would ultimately lead society to a grander outcome than the
one resulting from government planning and intervention. Central to
the thesis is the institution of the market, in which Adam Smith's
'unseen hand' operates. The doctrine alleges that it brings buyers and
sellers together in pursuit of their own self-interests so that individual
welfares, and the welfare of the whole of society, are simultaneously
maximized.

Implicit in Smith's system is a rejection of the intuition associated
with the logic of the commons. Recall that the commons in feudal
society was reserved for community use. It was not private property.
Rather, its purpose was somewhat akin to a modern park or recrea-
tion area. If a feudal serf threw his garbage on the commons, he
sacrificed the common good for his personal convenience. So long as
his anti-social behaviour did not become commonplace, the commons could support a small amount of garbage. But if such isolated
acts became commonplace and accepted as prudent by the masses – if
everyone threw his garbage on the commons – then society surely lost
because the commons became a garbage dump. And the individuals
who threw their garbage there also lost, because the normal use of
the commons was lost to them as well as to their neighbours.

A most unique character of Smith's philosophy is that it violates
that logic. Almost everyone perceives that collective action to control
selfish acts of individualism would enhance the commonweal. But
Smith argued counter-intuitively. His position was that individual
acts of selfishness could actually lead, through the market, to the
enhanced welfare of the individual and of society. Even when everyone acts in his own self-interest, the commonweal is enhanced more
than it would be through collective action imposed or coordinated by
government.

Increases in the 'wealth of nations' during the Industrial Revolution of the nineteenth century generally vindicated the efficacy of
Smith's claims. Self-interest became enshrined in America as both a
legal and an economic principle. And, except for an interlude during

the 1930s, economic policies based upon *laissez-faire* continued to perform well through the seventh decade of the twentieth century. But for over a decade now, the performance of the American economy has countermanded Smith's faith that independent and self-interested action would lead to a propitious outcome for society. It would appear that the logic of the commons has again become operative. Perhaps the world has changed so subtly that the self-interest which sparked the most dramatic economic progress in the history of the world, now often leads instead to injury to the collective well-being of society.

DISEQUILIBRIUM

It is asserted that the capitalist system broke down, beginning in the 1970s, because the nature of economic reality has changed. Doctrinaire capitalism therefore requires repair and modification, in a manner similar to the way in which economic theory was refurbished during and following the Great Depression.

For prescriptive theory to work adequately, it must account for the uniquenesses and the dynamisms that are present in the actual world. But conventional economics is based upon a natural law view which is antithetic to time or change, or anything akin to societal dynamism. Conventional theory is rooted in a natural law view that embodies the 'mechanics' of the seventeenth-century physical scientist Isaac Newton. Like Newton's vision of the heavens, economic theory assumes that some proper and perfect relationship exists between the economic whole and the sum of its parts. Economists portray the economic tableau in a state of equilibrium, in which friction and time are absent, and in which all economic adjustments are made instantaneously. Once attained, equilibrium is a condition in which all opposing forces are cancelled out, and the extant characteristics of the system are perpetuated from period to period.

The problem comes, then, in the application of an equilibrium-based theory to an actual economy. To the extent that conditions in an actual economy may not reflect the equilibrium conditions implicit in the natural law-based theoretical system, then accurate explanation and prediction of economic events will be frustrated. And if poor economic performance reveals Smith's assertion to be false – that the logic of the commons is actually operative in a society modelled upon *laissez-faire* principles – then some form of collective action is indicated. The ultimate goal of this book is to suggest principles of collective action that repair the *laissez-faire* system and restore its contemporary explanatory and predictive qualities.

LORD KEYNES

John Maynard Keynes is the economist who is associated with the repair of the intellectual apparatus following its debunking by the politically unacceptable outcomes of the Great Depression. His interest was in disequilibrium, and how the natural law-based intellectual system of his inheritance could be modified to improve its explanatory and predictive usefulness. Unfortunately, Keynes died at the end of the Second World War, rendering impossible any explanations he might have given for contemporary economic dysfunction.

Our quest is similar to Keynes's. It is to examine the possible linkage between contemporary dysfunction and the inability of the theoretical system to respond to disequilibrium in an actual economy. We shall see that disequilibrium may be revealed in a condition called hoarding, which is the retention of assets by wealth-holders in some non-productive use. During the Great Depression disequilibrium was revealed in the hoarding of gold. Wealth-holders who anticipated deflation found it to their best interest to hoard gold, rather than to place their wealth in current investment. A hoarding-induced reduction in the supply of money triggered the Depression era reduction of output and employment. Policies to dissuade hoarding, such as the repudiation of the International Gold Standard in 1933, and the outlawing of gold hoarding, were instrumental in moving the American economy back towards equilibrium.

Disequilibrium was manifested again during the 1970s as a response to inflation. Wealth-holders and speculators sought real estate and other inelastically supplied assets to avoid the ravages of currency depreciation. Hoarding real estate was generally more lucrative than investment placements. The outcome for the American economy was an inadequate supply of essential capital, which led to productivity declines, and ultimately to declining growth and the virtual attainment of stationary society.

Advocates of Reaganomics in 1981 argued that a tax cut to the wealthy, who are more likely to save than the poor, would stimulate saving and therefore investment in fixed capital. Buoyant growth would follow. But like Keynesian policies pursued during the 1970s, the managers of the economy failed to take account of disequilibrium hoarding behaviour. The tax cut coincided with actions which drove interest rates sharply higher.

Rather than place saving realized from the tax cut into tangible capital, many transactors opted for the security and profitability of financial instruments instead. Saving therefore became hoarded in finance and full employment equilibrium was not realized. The economic scenario which has thus emerged is more compatible with the vision of the neoclassical scholars – the stationary state – than it is compatible with the vision of Adam Smith. In the stationary state, net investment and profit are zero, and output and employment are stationary from period to period. The economy is moribund.

FINANCIAL HOARDING

A major thesis of this book is that finance-motivated behaviour reimposes the logic of the commons upon doctrinaire capitalism, thereby rendering the theory dysfunctional. Of particular concern is the 'profit lacuna' which was built into the intellectual system around the turn of the twentieth century by neoclassical economists. Because of the lacuna, the conventional model provides no reward to holding capital, and therefore no proffering of entrepreneurial skill and industry. The lacuna is manifested in the blurring of the distinction between capital and finance, and therefore between profit and interest.

If all economic activities earn the same rate of return, then the distinction between profit and interest is meaningless. Entrepreneurs would rather hold finance, all other things being equal, than hold capital, because holding the former is devoid of the costs of proffering skill or industry. It is also asserted that the world has changed subtly, making it possible for those who might otherwise hold capital, to hold finance instead, and with the same reward. The societal outcome of these combined phenomena – the profit lacuna and changes in the manner in which complex markets operate – is diminished investment and growth.

The complexity of the operation of 'real world' economies is not addressed by the neoclassical model – refurbished near the turn of this century – which is still in use. That model does not take account of the possible divisibility of tangible capital through leases and other mechanisms, of the creation of sophisticated markets for trading equity and finance, or of resource mobility which allows for international movement of tangible capital and finance. The outcome of these differences is that the contemporary entrepreneur may try to optimize the rate of return on finance, rather than the total profit on capital. Modern conglomerates and multinationals are examples of behaviour that is generally finance-motivated, rather than production, conservation and profit-motivated.

Mergers, acquisitions and other forms of finance-motivated endeavour are particularly important here. All these activities have as their end, not the creation of output, but the manipulation of ownership. Such manipulations and reorganizations can be terribly costly in human endeavour. They also frustrate productivity gains that might otherwise accrue to 'learning by doing'. The learning by doing hypothesis asserts that substantial productivity gains may accrue to a stable work environment as people learn to do their jobs with increasing efficiency, over time. A significant problem with continuous mergers and reorganizations is that they destabilize the productive environment, and therefore frustrate potential gains from learning by doing. As productivity lags, so also does economic growth.

Our proposal, then, is that the conventional economic theory must be patched or modified so that it can provide an effective guide for contemporary economies to approach equilibrium. By acknowledging the need for a theoretical patch, we also reject the denial by *laissez-faire* advocates of benefits to collective action. The particular kind of collective action proposed is called indicative economic planning. It has been practised most successfully by Japan since the Second World War.

America needs to overcome the 'financial leeching of capital' – particularly human capital, by providing incentives for investment, and disincentives for financial hoarding. Stronger incentives to encourage the provision of skill and industry should lead to improved conservation of tangible and human capital assets, to renewed stabilization of the productive environment, and to productivity gains through learning by doing.

To provide these incentives, it is first necessary for the American people to decide which assets they seek to conserve, and to expand. But it is not possible to specify the composition of capital unless the composition of future output is first specified. It is the contention of this book that the determination of future output, and therefore the specification of the composition of capital, should not be left to the vagaries of the free market. It should be determined by collective action.

Part II

The First Glitch of Economic Theory

Why Reaganomics and Keynesian Economics Failed is about the theoretical origins of contemporary economic dysfunction. Its ultimate focus is public policy: what must be done to overcome stationary society? Productivity problems may be caused by disinvestment. Rather than adding to the nation's stock of productively held assets, corporations and other organizations may undermine capital formation by engaging in finance-motivated practices.

To understand why the American economy isn't working properly, we first must understand subtleties of the intellectual apparatus that may decree it to be so. Part II discusses the first glitch of economic theory which is Say's Law: that supply creates its own demand, thereby equilibrating saving and investment. The intellectual origins of equilibrium analysis are the focus of Chapter 2, 'Isaac Newton and Economics'. Chapter 3 considers an alternative to conventional equilibrium analysis under the title 'A Disequilibrium View'.

2 Isaac Newton and Economics

Laissez-faire is the doctrine popularized by Adam Smith, the Scottish philosopher who wrote the *Wealth of Nations* in 1776. Literally interpreted, it means 'to let it be or to let go'. The eighteenth century was characterized by the rise of strong nation states in Western Europe. Within the context of the economic and political environment in which Smith lived, *laissez-faire* was an argument for keeping government out of the affairs of commerce.

Interest in *laissez-faire* during Smith's lifetime was a reaction against the growing influence of central governments in not only commerce, but in all aspects of human endeavour. According to Robert Clower (1974), former editor of the *American Economic Review*, Adam Smith lived in an age in which the traditional right of rulers to impose arbitrary and oppressive restrictions upon their subjects was coming under increasingly strong attack in all parts of the civilized world. Whereas other men might have conceived of an economy motivated by greed and controlled by a large number of uncoordinated agents as a recipe for chaos, Adam Smith argued that *laissez-faire* could and should replace government direction and regulation in affairs of production and trade.

NATURAL LAW

Smith's brilliant argument was based upon a *Weltanschauung* or world view that was very much like that of Isaac Newton's. The great physical scientist died in 1723, just four years after the birth of Adam Smith. According to Smith, the Newtonian system was the greatest discovery ever made by man. Newton saw the entire universe as governed by mechanical laws functioning with such precision that they could be formulated mathematically. He therefore sought to discover the principles governing the regularities of the physical universe, and give them expression in a system of natural laws.

Natural law is a study of the fundamental principles that order the universe and shape human nature. It posits that a universal or perfect order may exist in the world, that it is ultimately binding upon human society, that it can be discovered, and that living in harmony with that law insures maximum happiness. The pursuit of natural law is associated with the term 'moral philosophy'. Adam Smith held a chair by that name at the University of Glasgow. The *Encyclopedia Britannica*, published at Edinburgh in 1771 by 'A Society of Gentlemen in Scotland' during Smith's professoriate, defines moral philosophy as 'the study of manners or duty'.

One entered the university to study the universal or perfect order. Having done so, it therefore became obligatory upon the scholar to ask of his duty with regard to the promulgation of that order. The question, 'What ought I to do?' was perceived in two dimensions. The first pertained to the duty of the scholar *qua* individual. This is the agenda of individual/ethical inquiry. It asked the question, 'What is the responsibility of the individual?' The second pertained to collective action. It asked, 'What is the responsibility of society to the individual, particularly with regard to material well-being and social justice?' It is within this second context that the field of nineteenth-century political economy developed, and became differentiated from questions more precisely focused upon politics and law.

With his roots in the tradition of moral philosophy, then, Adam Smith attempted to discover the fundamental principles that he thought act universally upon the perceived life-blood of the social order – commerce – thereby effecting the wealth of nations. What ultimately gave his book lasting impact, according to Clower, was his conclusion that the economic activities of individuals could be more effectively coordinated through indirect and impersonal market forces which he characterized as natural forces, rather than through the actions of government policy.[1]

Since the nineteenth century, natural law theory has been largely displaced in economics and other social and natural sciences by scientific positivism based upon empirically derived facts. But notwithstanding modern method, we shall shortly observe that the underlying force of natural law yet governs the very foundations of conventional economic inquiry.

Smith and his followers, like his eminent teacher David Hume, sought to identify natural laws governing not only the behaviour of natural science, but the behaviour of economic society as well. The vision upon which his classical system was conceived portrayed economic transaction as a circulating phenomenon. This cosmography had its antecedents in the works of such pre-classical economists as Petty, Cantillon, and the French physiocrat François Quesnay. It was the latter who was also a physician serving in the court of Louis XV, and probably found the concept of circulating wealth analogous to the discovery, by the English anatomist William Harvey, of circulation of blood in the human body.

Rima (1978) points out that the term 'physiocracy' derives from the French word *physiocrate*, meaning 'rule of nature'. Quesnay was a believer in natural law: that the divine providence has ordained the existence of a universal and inherently perfect natural order, and that conformity to that order insures maximum human happiness. Wealth moves among transactors analogous to the way that blood moves among the organs of the body. Since economic activity is conceived as a circulating phenomenon, wealth, like Newton's view of matter, cannot be destroyed. Only the manifestation of wealth is changed through commerce.

EQUILIBRIUM

Newton's world view and the mathematical precision attached thereto, provided the classical economists and their physiocratic forebears with both a systematic conceptualization of commerce and a precise method for portraying it. It was based in an exposition of natural law. In a manner similar to the way the planets are stationary in their orbits, and their positions are therefore predictable from period to period, the analogous application of Newtonian mechanics to commerce offered both precision and order.

Implicit in the Newtonian system was the concept of equilibrium. In its use by eigteenth- and nineteenth-century physical scientists, it described a relationship between the whole and its parts in which opposing forces counterbalance each other. In the system of the classical economists, equilibrium was principally expressed as an outcome of the nullification of opposing market forces (Figure 2.1). Single-market equilibrium is the most demonstrative of its uses. Buyers seek low prices. The Law of Demand mandates that buyers demand smaller quantities at higher prices. Conversely, the Law of Supply states that sellers supply comparatively small quantities at low prices, and larger quantities at higher prices.

It is the price mechanism that rations market output. Many buyers and sellers, each acting in their own self-interest, bid the price up or down. At relatively high prices, sellers are willing to supply a larger quantity than buyers demand. This is called excess supply. And at

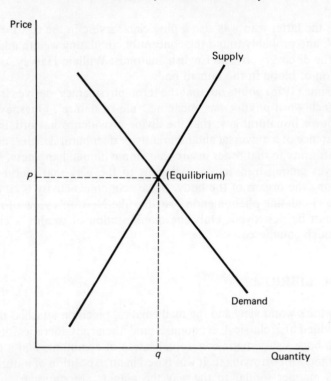

Figure 2.1   Market equilibrium for a single input or output

low prices the reverse is true: excess demand prevails. It is only at the prevailing equilibrium price p, and quantity q, which is sought after and established by the impersonal coordination forces of the market, that excess demand and excess supply are zero. At equilibrium the prevailing price and quantity variables remain constant from period to period until a change may occur in the demand or supply schedules, or functions of buyers or sellers.[2]

General or systematic equilibrium prevails throughout an economy when excess demand and excess supply are absent from all its markets – both input and output – simultaneously. Much of the elegance of the Newtonian method derives from its symmetry, which lends itself nicely to the elegant and abstract manipulations of mathematics. General equilibrium received its most sophisticated treatment in the nineteenth century at the hand of Léon Walras. According to G. L. S. Shackle (1958), it offered the wonderful power to calculate and predict the movements of celestial bodies, which had come from the work of Galileo, Kepler and Newton . . . The influence of this thought has worked an increasing strength in economics and is seen at its height in the work of the econometric model builders.

Shackle further points out that the Walras–Pareto formulation excludes time and everything that belongs to time including growth, invention and innovation. We shall presently observe this to be a most telling outcome.

The use of general equilibrium analysis released its most conceptual manipulators from the otherwise messy and often intractable problems of specifying systemic characteristics in disequilibrium. To study a hypothetical economy in disequilibrium would be tantamount to hypothesizing some perturbation of nature in which natural order is momentarily suppressed and chaos prevails. Such is the case for the presence of friction or time in an otherwise frictionless and timeless state. The existence of disequilibrium conditions, of course, are inconsistent with the orderly cosmography which the classics sought to portray.

In the primal paradigm of classical economics, wealth (defined as current income) flows in a circuit between the two 'organs' of the system – households and firms. Thus, the resource expenditures of the business sector become the income receipts of the household sector (Figure 2.2). And the value of goods and services supplied to households is identically offset by the revenues for those goods and services provided by households to businesses. This is a systematic manifestation of equilibrium in an economy, and it is a tautology. It is true by definition, just as assets must always equal liabilities plus net worth on an organization's balance sheet. Current wealth – which is now called national income – never leaves the system. It is neither created nor destroyed in this equilibrium formulation. It is merely transferred among transactors.

We must reiterate that the time period of adjustment in the classical system is instantaneous. A set of 'false' prices never prevails in the *laissez-faire* formulation wherein all markets may not clear within the market period. Time and friction do not exist. Opposing forces within the competitive model are marshalled virtually instantaneously. Typically, the contemporary analyst using this orthodox method assumes that an actual economy should operate according to

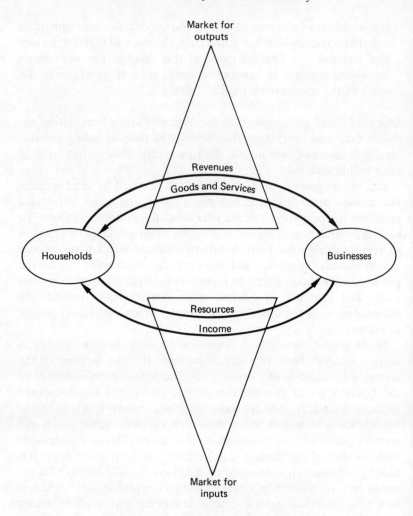

Figure 2.2 Systemic equilibrium

this natural law archetype and that it obtains equilibrium essentially continuously, but surely within some fixed interval accounting period such as a month, a calendar quarter or a fiscal year. However, there may exist dramatic divergence between this abstract method, embodying a natural law cosmography, and an actual economy.

THE GREAT DEPRESSION

The occurrence of the Great Depression challenged the applicability of the Newtonian instantaneous equilibrating mechanism to the 'real world'. The precipitating cause of the Depression was the stock market collapse of October 1929. Productivity weaknesses and near-feverish speculation in land and common stocks preceded the crash, and had characterized the American economy in the latter part of the decade. Much of the speculation was financed by highly leveraged transactions. Stock traders often made purchases on precarious margins. Banks typically accepted stock as collateral for loans to buy more stock – loaning up to as much as 80 or 90 per cent of market value. When tremors began to erode the unbounded optimism of the market, profit-taking ensued. Many traders were wiped out as the market fell precipitously. And along with their financial ruin also came the financial ruin of many lending institutions which were left holding undervalued collateral. Huge bank losses mounted. As an increasing quantity of bank loans became subject to call, the quantity of money in circulation shrank dramatically.

However, the stock market rebounded, beginning in December 1929, following the October crash. But between September 1930 and June 1932 the market fell again by 80 per cent, to its lowest level during the Depression. Saint-Etienne (1984) points out that what is less well known is that the stock of money remained almost unchanged until April 1930, and fell only marginally in the year following. Then, between March 1931 and March 1933, the transactions component of the money supply contracted by 22 per cent, and 'broad money' (transactions component plus saving accounts and time deposits) contracted by 30 per cent.

Financial instability quickly led to destabilization of the private sector as consumer spending flagged, production was cut, and unemployment mounted. Although the rate of unemployment has been calculated differently since the Second World War, it is estimated that joblessness reached 25 per cent of the labour force by 1933. Between 1929 and 1933 the real value of gross national product fell by 30 per cent, and did not regain the output level first attained in 1929 until ten years later, in spite of a 15 per cent increase in the size of the labour force during that period.

In defence of what John Kenneth Galbraith calls the prevailing 'conventional wisdom', the economic orthodoxy appealed for time (the 'long run') and the continuing absence of government intervention, in which full employment equilibrium might again be obtained. But the British political economist John Maynard Keynes, who published *The General Theory* in 1936, contended that unemployment could long endure, which was a politically untenable situation. He argued that 'In the long run we are all dead'. What he meant was that actual economies may not be disposed to behave consistently with the eighteenth-century 'Camelot' natural law view of instantaneous equilibration. Friction and time may enter into the 'real world', thereby requiring that the predictive basis of Newtonian-oriented theory be adjusted to account for the lack of articulation between the plans of buyers and sellers. In the United States, Keynes' intellectual position was pragmatically implemented three years before the appearance of *The General Theory* (1936) with the 'New Deal' of Franklin D. Roosevelt.

According to Keynes, full employment equilibrium is more likely to be the exception than the rule. Economic society may become 'stuck' indefinitely at a level of output and employment which is an equilibrium level, but insufficient to provide a politically viable level of prosperity. In so arguing, Keynes rejected what is called Say's Law. Its simplistic interpretation is that supply creates its own demand. A more sophisticated interpretation of the meaning of Say's Law is that the production of current period output simultaneously generates a flow of income sufficient to purchase that output. It is a condition for the occurrence of systemic equilibrium.

Say's Law may be more appropriately described as a tautology than a law. In fact, it is a prescription for the imposition of the equilibrium condition of natural law upon the workings of an extant economy. Since friction and time do not exist in the world of natural law, any real economy modelled upon its precepts should expect to obtain equilibrium in any accounting period in which that economy may be observed, such as a fiscal year. By rejecting Say's Law, then, Keynes acknowledged that an actual economy may not conform to the highly restrictive assumptions of natural law which portend instantaneous equilibration.[3]

Keynes died in 1946, leaving his followers the task of 'operationalizing' his modifications to the conventional doctrine. Those who followed after him, including Sir John Hicks of Cambridge and Alvin Hansen of Harvard, created a deterministic mathematical system and a predictive science on the basis of the rather tortured and indeterminate system contained in Keynes's Depression era treatise. It is this 'Keynesian' system that became the prototype for American economic policy through the 1970s. We shall therefore attempt to distinguish between what Keynes may have actually meant, and the Keynesian system that attempts to translate the nuance of Keynes's complex book into a general system for managing economic health.

KEYNESIAN ECONOMICS

Lord Keynes didn't actually reject the natural law basis of conventional economic analysis. Indeed, he was trained as a 'neoclassical' or new classical economist under the tutelage of the great Cambridge scholar, Alfred Marshall. What he attempted to demonstrate was how an actual economy might depart from the Camelot adjustment mechanism of natural law. His solution was not to make a discontinuous break with convention. Rather, his perspective was that of a reformer arguing that conventional analysis was vital, but that the policy conclusions flowing from it must be mitigated and tempered by acknowledging differences that might exist between an actual economy and the natural law archetype. Taking account of critical differences allows the policy analyst to benefit from the richness of the conventional theory without losing sight of the limits of its applicability.

Standard textbook assessments of the contribution of John Maynard Keynes are based upon quantitative reconstructions of the neoclassical system which Keynes criticized, but these are modified to account for his criticisms. According to an assessment of the professional literature by Aschheim and Hsieh (1969), only three differences are revealed in the formal (mathematical) structures of the Keynesian and neoclassical systems. The neoclassical reformulation of classical economic thought began in the 1870s.

First, Keynes rejected the neoclassical supply of labour function that posits a perfectly competitive and instantaneously adjusting labour market. Rather than cutting the price of their labour – the wage rate – in order to provide employment for everyone (by reducing their wages until the quantity of labour that workers wish to supply is equal to the quantity that employers which to purchase), workers may band together into trade unions to oppose wage reductions. Keynes did not oppose labour unions or other utility-maximizing behaviours by workers, even though their actions are at variance with the natural law view. Rather, he argued that labour market behaviours in an actual economy are divergent from the

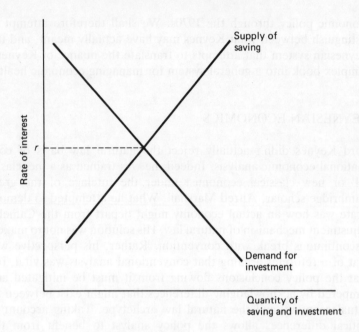

Figure 2.3   Market for loanable funds

vision of the neoclassical system which assumes wage and price flexibility. Therefore, an actual economy may obtain equality between saving and investment, in Keynes' view, but at a relatively high wage rate and at a low quantity of labour traded, and thus at a level of national income insufficient to support full employment.

Second, Keynes added to the neoclassical system a speculative demand for money function. This means that transactors are alleged to hold money for reasons other than as a means of exchange only. In anticipation of a decline in prices (deflation), some transactors may convert their assets into money. Money may become a speculative device since certain quantities of it may be held specifically to fulfil a profit-taking motive.

Third, Keynes assumed that income is the primary determinant of saving. This is contrasted with the neoclassical view that the interest rate equilibrates saving and investment. The hypothesized neoclassical market for loanable funds is illustrated in Figure 2.3. Note that households (which undertake all saving in the simplified two-sector model) are induced to save more as interest rates rise. Conversely, businesses (which undertake all investment) are induced to invest more only as interest rates fall. The interest rate is therefore the price of borrowed money (borrowed from households by businesses for investment). Free market forces in the neoclassical model are assumed to drive the interest rate to that level at which equality exists between the quantity of saving supplied and the quantity of investment demanded. Equilibrium is thereby assured.

Equality between saving and investment is the principle vehicle by which Newtonian mechanics is portrayed in modern employment theory. It is only when all current household saving is translated into current period investment that the rate of growth of national output is unchanged from period to period, which is a description of equilibrium. In the Keynesian system it is only possible to apply his analysis and to observe an extant economy when it fulfils the likeness of the vision of natural law. It must be in equilibrium – wherein there is equality between saving and investment – for economic analysis to proceed.

Neoclassical economists had asserted that the normal equilibrating movement of the interest rate in the market for loanable funds would insure continuous equality between household saving and business investment. And, with flexible wages as well as flexible prices for producer goods and services, they further assumed that equilibrium would occur at full employment, wherein everyone who wants to work is able to find work.

Contrary to the self-regulating model described in Figure 2.3, Keynes argued that businesses do not borrow solely because the interest rate is low. In fact they may borrow even at comparatively high interest rates so long as expected revenues resulting from investment exceed the expected costs of borrowed money. It is profitability, then, rather than the comparatively low price of money alone, which motivates businesses to borrow for investment.

Of course, we have mentioned earlier Keynes's argument that households save for reasons other than to obtain interest. Saving, it was hypothesized by Keynes, is undertaken for retirement, for the purchase of consumer durables such as cars and appliances, to reconcile receipts with purchases (cash flow management), and the like. Consequently, it is not the rate of interest but the level of income that determines the amount saved by households. At higher levels of income, members of society are able to withhold more total dollars from consumption and channel them into saving. But Keynes argued that saving as a proportion of changes in national income was a stable function.

Now, we may ask the question, 'What if inflexible wages and prices prevent equilibrium from occurring at the full employment level of output (the level of GNP necessary to provide employment for everyone choosing to work in an extant economy)?' The neoclassical economists argued that time and government restraint would provide the appropriate environment in which businesses would eventually cut prices in order to liquidate excess inventory, and households would lower their reservation wages in order to obtain work for all. The public policy cure for depression or recession was straight-forward. The conventional wisdom argued that it was expedient to wait until natural market forces brought conditions in extant economies into compliance with the assumptions of the doctrinal *laissez-faire* system based upon natural law.

The Keynesian argument, on the other hand, is far less sanguine. It asserts that an actual economy could obtain equilibrium between business investment and household saving at a quantity of national income insufficient to insure everyone a job. Worse yet, declining wages and incomes could provoke a downward spiral in which business investment is continuously reduced in anticipation of ever-declining receipts. Further, pursuing public policies to motivate workers and businesses to endure wage and price cuts would only further provoke the downward spiral.

KEYNESIAN EQUILIBRIUM

Since the quantity of saving (and therefore consumption) is determinant for any given level of national income if we know the consumption or saving schedules of an extant economy, we can graphically portray the Newtonian equilibrating mechanism in the Keynesian system. Note that the saving function in Figure 2.4 is a straight, upward-sloping line. The implication is that economic society will save (and therefore consume, also) some constant portion of increases or decreases in national income. In the Keynesian jargon this constancy between changes in consumption or saving resulting from changes in national income is called the marginal propensity to consume or the marginal propensity to save, respectively. Again, the practical significance in Keynesian theory is that it is income, and not the rate of interest, that determines the levels of consumption and saving.

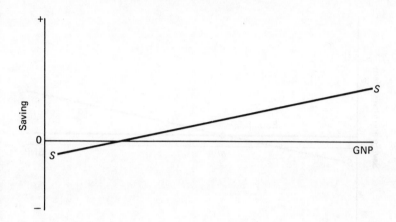

Figure 2.4   Society's national output determines its level of saving

Of course, saving and investment equality is the condition for equilibrium, which is a requirement of the conventional method. Only when the business sector undertakes an amount of investment precisely equal to the amount of saving in the household sector can equilibrium be obtained. If these are not equal, then national income would be increasing or decreasing from period to period. Recall that equilibrium is a condition from which there is no tendency to change: no opposing forces work against the perpetuation of the status quo.

We describe saving in the Keynesian formulation as 'endogenous'. This is a compact way to state that saving (and consumption) is determinant in the Keynesian system if income is known. Business investment, on the other hand, is 'exogenous'. It is not determined by the level of income, but rather by expectations of profitability by the business sector.

Expectation is a key word here. Keynes emphasized that it was the expected marginal efficiency of capital – the difference between expected net revenues and the expected costs of finance – that determines business investment. In the Keynesian formulation, the investment function is a straight line conveying the assumption that the business sector plans to invest some constant amount in the relevant period. It is constant, *ex post* (viewed from after the fact), because the level of commitment was chosen *ex ante* (the planning horizon), before national income for the period was known.

Equilibrium may occur at any point along the saving function(s) in

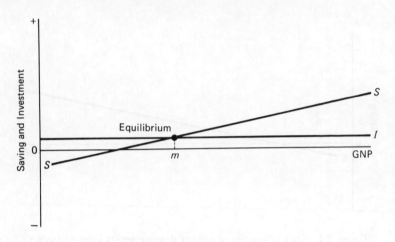

Figure 2.5　The equilibrium level of national output is determined by saving
　　　　　　equality with investment

Figures 2.4 or 2.5. Since investment is determined exogenously, it is
the variable that determines the level of national income in the
Keynesian system. Alternately stated, an economy creates that
amount of national income that is determined by the amount of
investment undertaken in the business sector. The Keynesian system
for determining national income is driven by the quantity of investment, which, in turn, is driven by business expectations of the
profitability of capital investment. In Keynes's system there is no
provision for the articulation of the saving plans of households with
the investment plans of businesses. Therefore, it is only by sheer
coincidence that saving and investment may be in equality.

Now we are prepared to consider the economic policy ramifications
of the Keynesian system. Its policy focus is to explain and to cure
national income shortfalls, or economic gluts. These are presumed to
be caused by a drop in exogenous investment below the full employment level. It would be appealing, of course, if the business sector
could be motivated, *ex ante*, to increase its investment to the full
employment level. But since business investment is motivated by
profitability, this is unlikely.

According to Keynes, it is the responsibility of a third sector that
does not appear in the *laissez-faire* formulation – government – to
make up any anticipated investment shortfall. It may do so through
selling bonds to finance the investment stimuli, which is deficit

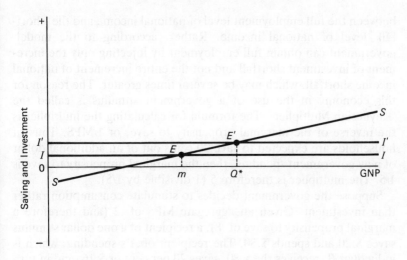

Figure 2.6   The government obtains full employment at Q* by providing the difference in investment between I and I'

financing. Alternately, it can be demonstrated that the government may also obtain the same results through any form of new government spending, whether that spending may be undertaken to obtain private or public capital, or to directly stimulate citizen consumption.

Note in Figure 2.6 that saving and investment equality occurs initially at point E which corresponds with GNP level M. Since this is not the full employment level of national income that is created in the production of current GNP, new government spending in the amount of I' minus I is initiated, to reach equilibrium at the full employment level, $Q*$.

KEYNESIAN POLITICS

The economic and political philosophy that is generated from Keynesian analysis is a stark contrast to the non-interventionist posture of *laissez-faire*. Keynesians advocate what has been called 'functional finance', which differs dramatically from the cyclically or annually balanced budget. Government becomes the guarantor of full employment by undertaking spending that is sufficient to compensate for any shortfall in business investment.

It is not necessary for the government to inject the entire difference between the full employment level of national income and the 'short-fall' level of national income. Rather, according to the model, government can obtain full employment by injecting only the increment of investment shortfall and not the entire increment of national income shortfall, which may be several times greater. The reason for this economy in the use of a government stimulus is called the 'Keynesian Multiplier'. The formula for calculating the multiplier is the inverse of the marginal propensity to save, or 1/MPS. Thus, if households are expected to save 20 cents out of an additional dollar of new government spending, then the marginal propensity to save is 1/5. The multiplier is therefore 5 (1 divisible by 1/5).

Suppose the government decides to stimulate consumption rather than investment. Given an aggregate MPS of .2 (and therefore a marginal propensity to save of .8), a recipient of a one dollar stimulus saves $.20 and spends $.80. The recipient of A's spending, which is individual B, receives the $.80, saves 20 per cent or $.16, and in turn spends 80 per cent or $.64 with C, and so on. Obviously the cumulative impact of the stimulus grows far beyond its initial value. If we continued our calculations, we should find that $5 of new national income is generated from the $1 initial injection. The initial injection is multiplied by a factor of 5 in this example, because the MPS is .2. In reality economic researchers report the recent value of the Keynesian multiplier to be in a range between about 2 and 2.5.

It is important to acknowledge that the Keynesian system is demand driven and that it is explanatory of economic gluts. It assumes that economic society is operating inside its 'Production Possibilities Frontier'. Such a point is demonstrated in Figure 2.7. Along the frontier are points representing various quantities of two goods, food and clothing, in a simplified two good illustration. Each point on the curve represents full employment and the utilization of contemporary technology. It is possible for society, in this illustration, to choose to forego a point on the frontier, say point A, and the quantities of food and clothing associated with it, for another point, say point B, associated with different quantities of the two goods. The exact location on the frontier is a choice of society. However, if national output shifts downward and to the left, say to point C, then at that point society is operating inefficiently because unemployment and excess capacity prevail. Existing resources could be used to provide more of either or both goods.

Keynesian analysis focuses upon the problems and solutions re-

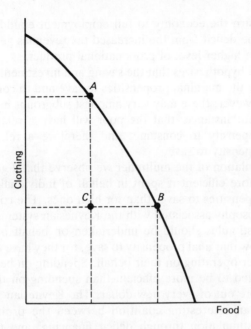

Figure 2.7 At full employment, society may choose any point along the
production possibilities frontier

quired to move from a point inside the production possibilities
frontier to a point on the frontier. The system is oriented to rectifying
demand deficiencies. Keynesian policies do not effect supply: that is,
they do not directly augment resources or technology and therefore
they are not designed to shift the frontier outward over time, which is
a formal definition of the growth of economic capacity. Keynesian
economics is not capable of offering insight into how to obtain
economic growth under conditions of full employment. Its value is
that of obtaining the limits of economic capacity under conditions of
economic glut.

With regard to the multiplier, then, the Keynesian system can
hypothetically create an increase in national income, moving towards
the full employment level, that may be substantially greater than the
government stimulus necessary to obtain it. Once full employment is
obtained, the logic assumes that it will be maintained under normal,
continuing circumstances. Thus, an original political appeal of
Keynesian arguments was that government could undertake a deficit

stimulus, return the economy to full employment equilibrium, and then repay the deficit from the increased tax revenues generated by producing the higher level of gross national product.

The system hypothesizes that the saving and investment functions, and therefore the marginal propensities to save and to consume, are constant. However, these may vary amongst subgroups in society. It is assumed, for instance, that the poor will have a relatively high marginal propensity to consume, and therefore a relatively low marginal propensity to save.

In the calculation of the multiplier we observe that a government stimulus is more efficient if spent in behalf of individuals with low marginal propensities to save, than for high ones. The conventional political philosophy associated with the Keynesian system is that the government stimulus should be undertaken on behalf of the poor who have a low marginal propensity to save, for they have a relatively high multiplier operating on their behalf. Spending on behalf of the poor is asserted to be more efficient than spending on the affluent who save more out of every new dollar. The Keynesian system has perpetuated an interesting coalition between the proponents of government stimulation through deficit financing, and the proponents of government-backed initiatives to improve the standard of living of poor citizens.

FALLACY OF SAVING

The Keynesian prescription for economic health is clear. It is for the government to undertake deficit-financed spending to countermand unemployment by propelling the economy back to its equilibrium level of full employment on the production possibilities frontier. We have briefly discussed precipitating causes of unemployment associated with economic gluts, and concluded that gluts are portrayed in the Keynesian system primarily by a downward shift in the investment function.

Alternately, a glut could also be portrayed by a backward shift in the saving function. As Figure 2.8 demonstrates, the saving function has shifted backwards from SS to $S'S'$, and therefore we conclude that the consumption function has shifted forwards. At any level of GNP the quantity of saving is now greater than prior to the shift. Equality between saving and investment is now obtained at a lower level of GNP than before. Since the saving function is endogenous

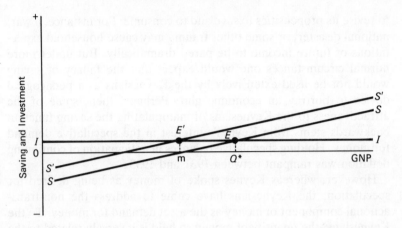

Figure 2.8   An increase in saving causes a decline in GNP: the paradox of thrift

and not likely to shift outwards, a remedial increase in government investment or other spending is indicated to move back to full employment equilibrium.

The fallacy of saving in the Keynesian system which is an application of the logic of the commons, infers that while increased saving out of current income may benefit the future consumption of a single individual, that when it is attempted by everyone simultaneously, the aggregate level of future income actually falls. So, while it may appear expedient for a single individual to save more out of current income during a glut, the aggregate outcome is a decline in the future living standard.

But why does Keynesian analysis devote substantial attention to the fallacy of saving when a backward shift in the saving function violates the assumption that the consumption and saving functions are stable? To obtain insight into this 'curiousm', we must begin by reiterating the characteristics of the conventional method. Keynes used the comparative static method of analysis. It can only be applied to an extant economy if that economy is assumed to be in equilibrium, wherein saving is equal to investment. Recall also that investment is the exogenous variable which determines the level of national income.

If we choose to portray an economic glut in the Keynesian system through a backward shift in the saving function, we might presume that some 'shock' has occurred to the household sector that causes it to revise its propensities to save and to consume. For instance, a war, national disaster, or some other trauma may cause household expectations of future income to be pared dramatically. But under more normal circumstances one would expect that the fallacy of saving would not be used extensively by the Keynesians as a pedagogical device to portray an economic glut. Perhaps, then, some of the attractiveness to the Keynesians of manipulating the saving function backwards stems from Keynes's interest in the speculative demand for money. Holding speculative balances in anticipation of continuing deflation was rampant between 1931 and 1933.

However, whereas Keynes spoke of money as being desired for speculation, the Keynesians have come to address the non-transactional component of money as the asset demand for money. To the Keynesians, the quantity of money so held is inversely related to the rate of interest. Presumably, at high rates of interest the opportunity cost of holding money as an asset is high, and therefore the asset demand for money is low, since households seek earnings from holding interest-bearing near-monies. Consequently, comparatively low rates of interest are associated with low opportunity cost. Transactors are alleged to hold a larger quantity of money at low interest rates because the placement of wealth in 'the next best use' rather than money is not so compelling.

We must acknowledge that money was very different in the 1930s than it is today. Contemporary money is fiat money. It has transaction value by virtue of government decree, and it has no intrinsic value. The money stock of the early Depression, however, was gold or was convertible into gold. It had intrinsic value. As the money supply shrank dramatically between 1931 and 1933, the value of the dollar rose as speculation in gold, which we shall call hoarding, became rampant in anticipation that the dollar would continue to appreciate.

Keynesians are hard pressed to explain the hoarding of gold. Note the Keynesian asset demand for money function portrayed in Panel *B* of Figure 2.9. In it, the quantity of money held in asset balances is inversely related to the prevailing rate of interest. Interest rates did fall as the Depression solidified. But there is little historical evidence that gold was being hoarded because of low interest rates. We therefore conclude that there is a substantial difference between the demand for contemporary fiat money as an asset, and the demand for gold money as a speculative device during panics, when the value of money is rising.

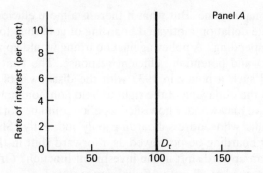

Transactions demand for money

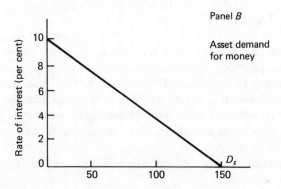

Figure 2.9   Transactions demand and asset demand for money

The saving function in the Keynesian system is shifted backwards to a lower level of national income, as described in Figure 2.9. This realignment may occur in the Keynesian system because of a shift in the household saving and consumption schedules, in spite of Keynes's assertion that these tend to be invariant. What the Keynesians actually accomplish with the portrayal of the fallacy of saving is to represent changes in the consumption and saving functions that might result, not from a drop in the rate of interest, but from increased hoarding activity. Hoarding appears to be smuggled into the Keynesian analysis by making the asset demand for money an increasing function of the decreasing rate of interest.

The conventional Keynesian policy prognostication for eliminating the hoarding of money is to increase investment so that it again equilibrates with the higher level of saving at the full employment level of national income. But what if there is a more efficient way to respond to the deflation-motivated hoarding of gold than to increase government spending? A policy against hoarding would appear to be a more direct and potentially efficient response. The United States implemented such a policy in 1933 with the disavowal of the gold standard and the outlawing of the right to hold non-nominal amounts of gold. But we may wonder how such a policy could be portrayed by the Keynesians who address hoarding only indirectly. Should the regulation of hoarding be portrayed as a forward shift in the saving function, or an upward shift in the investment function? Or, indeed, can it be portrayed at all in the Keynesian system?

A MONETARIST VIEW

Apart from neoclassical and Keynesian analyses, the monetarist school has provided a substantial explanation of the causes and possible cures of the Great Depression. Rather than dealing with 'real' variables such as saving and investment and their impact upon GNP, the monetarists study the relationship between the quantity of money in circulation and GNP. This relationship is portrayed in 'the equation of exchange'.

The equation can be divided into a 'money' side and an 'output' side:

Money side		*Output side*
Money × Velocity	=	Price level × Output
$(M) \times (V)$	=	$(P) \times (Q)$

M is the average quantity of money in circulation for the year, and V is the number of times the 'average' dollar is employed to purchase final goods and services during the year. Q is the value of final output, or GNP. P is the price level or 'numeraire'. As it increases (or decreases) with regard to some fixed quantity of Q, the value of money therefore decreases (or increases). As a simplification we consider only the relationship between money and current production. We omit the relationship between money and the value of second-hand goods traded in the economy, financial transactions such as the buying and selling of stocks and bonds, and the purchase and sale of 'intermediate goods' that are resold and ultimately combined into final output.

The monetarists believe that money and monetary policy are more important determinants of national income than investment. They argue that *V*, the velocity of circulation, is essentially stable. If *V* is held constant in the theoretical equation of exchange, then the causal implications of money upon the money value of GNP in an extant economy become apparent. With velocity constant, an increase in *M* results in an increase in *PQ*, which is the money or nominal value of GNP. Under conditions of full employment and therefore a constant *Q*, increases in *M* will be revealed as increases in the price level. We recognize this as inflation. However, if *Q* lies below its full employment level, then monetarists presume that an increase in the stock of money will be revealed through an increase in *Q* rather than an increase in *P*.

Monetarists argue that the Great Depression was a monetary phenomenon. The collapse of the stock market led to a condition which dramatically shrank the supply of money in circulation. Part of this shrinkage can be explained by a withdrawal of gold into speculative hoards, or by the 'money-destroying' impact of massive defaults on bank loans. According to the monetarists, prosperity could have been restored through the action of the monetary authority during that period to motivate the private banking system to create new loans, and therefore to add to the supply of money. Instead, the Federal Reserve did virtually nothing to accelerate money growth. Keynesian policies that were undertaken in the United States after 1933, to stimulate aggregate spending toward the full employment level, are viewed by monetarists merely as a means of getting new money into circulation.

Effective Keynesian stimulation policies do normally depend upon accommodative money-creating measures. Otherwise, new government spending would strain the existing money supply, if velocity holds constant. The result could be a 'crowding out' of private businesses from borrowing in the money market. As the transactions demand for money increases with public spending and national income expansion, the interest rate in the market for loanable funds rises to ration scarce dollars, thereby curtailing private borrowing.

So the monetarist appraisal of the Keynesian system is that it works principally because it is an indirect approach to getting more money into circulation. Keynesians counter the monetarist argument that it is possible for only some specific quantity of money to support a particular output and price level combination. They argue that velocity may speed up (or slow down) to accommodate changing levels of national income in the presence of a constant money supply.

The conflict between the explanatory value of Keynesian and

monetarist views would appear to be resolvable by appealing empirically to the velocity of circulation. The monetarists would expect V to be quite stable, whereas the Keynesians would expect it to be quite volatile. Actually, the evidence demonstrates a reasonably close correlation between long-term movements between M and PQ, thereby supporting a fairly stable role for V. The evidence also suggests that V is not nearly as stable as the monetarists theoretically assert. Neither side appears to win the debate clearly with regard to the causes and cures of the Great Depression.

A MYSTERY VARIABLE?

Is it possible that both the monetarist and the Keynesian systems for determining national income have failed to recognize some 'mystery' variable that is correlated both with declining investment as well as with declining stocks of gold-backed money in circulation? If a 'mystery variable' did exist that could link monetarist and Keynesian explanations, what might it be? And how might it have been overlooked in both systems?

Perhaps the two theoretical explanations might find some connection through the speculative demand for money which is 'bastardized' into the asset demand for money in the Keynesian system. For instance, if we could 'disconnect' the Keynesian asset demand for money function from the rate of interest, we could then explore a rationale for hoarding gold during the Depression which is not correlative with the rate of interest.

So, what variable, as yet unaccounted, might be related to the hoarding of gold? We have observed that the prevailing methodology precludes the acknowledgement of any disequilibrium variable. Perhaps this is the reason why Keynesians confuse the asset demand for money with Keynes's speculative demand for money. We might ask, then, what alterations in economic method must occur to allow the economic tableau to be viewed in some condition other than equilibrium?

3 A Disequilibrium View

In his preface to *The General Theory* Keynes agonized over his 'long struggle to escape . . . from habitual modes of thought and expression'. The difficulty, he said, 'lies, not in the new ideas, but in escaping from the old ones, which ramify, for those brought up as most of us have been, into every corner of our minds'. It was the conventional wisdom of his time that Keynes attacked. Its inability to correct economic dysfunction, coupled with the heroic attempts of its defenders to shelter it from criticism, had led to what Keynes observed to be 'deep divergences of opinion' among the professional economists of his time.

In his criticism of the neoclassical system, Keynes did not discard the intellectual heritage of his mentors and opponents. Indeed, his method was that of his Cambridge mentor, Alfred Marshall. It is called comparative static analysis, and is used to explain and predict the behaviours of an actual economy through a series of observations promulgated on the heroic assumption that each observation coincides with equilibrium. The method is somewhat analogous to flipping through a deck of still photographs to stimulate the changes of passing time. Each portrait portrays its subject in a state of equilibrium, or 'ideal repose'. As the subject ages, and other changes take place over time, these are recorded at the appropriate intervals selected by the photographer. Later, movement can be simulated by animating the deck of photographs in the manner described.

But time is never portrayed directly, either in this analogy or in comparative static analysis. Conventional economic analysis – even in the Keynesian system – is not capable of actually viewing an extant economy in disequilibrium. Indeed, the method abhors time and therefore disequilibrium, for these are at variance with the vision of the natural order which portrays society as operating under continuous conditions of harmony and order. We can only wonder, then, at the events that might have occurred between portrait sittings, as these events may have shaped the outcomes which we behold. In fact the comparative static method is one of marvellous concealment! We could learn so much more about our subject if we could capture movement with time's passage, thereby allowing the subject to be 'on camera' continuously in both times of flux as well as times of ideal repose.

TIME IN ECONOMICS

Keynes's rejection of Say's Law necessitated the introduction of time and friction into the economic intercourse of households and businesses. Keynes attempted to do so, although his method was incomplete and the mechanics of his analysis were flawed. In the end, Keynes was less than completely successful in his long struggle to escape. Since he never confronted disequilibrium directly, he could only posit that it might occur between equilibria. Saving must always equal investment in the comparative static methodology. But in Keynes's system, he differentiated between *ex post* and *ex ante* equality between saving and investment. *Ex post*, or viewed from a historical perspective, saving must always equal investment. This is Say's Tautology.

But, *ex ante* – for instance at the beginning of a fiscal year – it would be possible to predict whether equilibrium at year's end will coincide with a rate of output similar to that which prevailed at the year's beginning. If we look, *ex ante*, at the plans of households and businesses and find them to be unsyncronized, we may conclude that saving and investment inequality will lead to a change in the rate of output during the period. We infer that for such a change to occur disequilibrium must prevail during the period.

For instance, if businesses plan to invest less in the next fiscal year than households plan to save in that period, then the economy will be operating at a lower rate of output than the rate of output prevailing at our initial equilibrium observation. Since planned saving exceeds planned investment, it is assumed that businesses will be liquidating inventories and laying off labour, and that households will be reducing their consumption levels, until the endogenous level of saving is equal with the exogenous level of investment for the period.

One wonders how the analyst can foresee when an equilibrium observation will next occur following a period of instability. Specifically, can we be sure that equilibrium will always prevail at year's end? Might it not be feasible instead for end-of-year *ex post* analysis to reveal the rate of saving to be higher than the rate of investment? Actually, in the Keynesian system equilibrium is typically 'invoked' at the end of the fiscal year. In spite of Keynes's acknowledgement of *ex ante* disequilibrium, the Keynesian analyst assumes that an actual economy obtains *ex post* equilibrium essentially continuously – in conformity with the vision of the natural order – but surely within some fixed interval accounting period such as a fiscal year.[1]

Of course, there may exist a dramatic divergence between this abstract method embodying the natural law cosmography and the equilibrating mechanism of an actual economy. The problem is obvious. It is one thing to portray an extant economy as a self-regulating, circulating system; but it is quite another arbitrarily to decree that it must be in *ex post* equilibrium each and every time we may choose to study it. It would appear to constitute the ultimate act of hubris in economics to assume that an actual economy shall be in equilibrium whenever we may choose to study it.

Even though Keynes struggled to acknowledge the effects of time, he never disavowed the Newtonian cosmography as it operates in conventional theory, declaring that the world acts in an orderly manner. He never completely separated conditions in an extant economy, in which disequilibrium may prevail, from the natural law archetype which decrees equality between saving and investment to be the 'normal state of affairs'.

The problem of applying such a neat system of intellectual intrigue to an actual economy is that it justifies the practice of taking 'snapshots' of economic indicators at arbitrary fixed intervals and then venerating those snapshots as representations of the fulfilment of the Newtonian equilibrium condition. It is one thing to portray an actual economy as a self-regulating, circulating system; but it is quite another to decree that it must continuously fulfil that condition.

THE KEYNESIAN OMISSION

Keynes's method for acknowledging the presence of time and friction – which allows the equilibrating condition of the Camelot order to be suspended temporarily through *ex ante* analysis – is little different from and ultimately not too much more insightful than the method of Keynes's mentors. The very act of invoking conventional analysis – even with Keynes's *ex ante* modification – obliterates any view of extant disequilibria. Saving and investment become cast as tautologically equal in the period ending with the invocation.

Investment is measured directly in the national income accounts. Saving, however, is calculated indirectly, and is the residual or 'leftover' of income after accounting directly for consumption, taxes and the like. Saving and investment, of course, can only be the same value in equilibrium. Since saving is never observed directly, it can be manipulated marginally by the way the data are collected so that the equilibrium condition of saving equality with investment is generally fulfilled.

Keynes acknowledged the difference between the perfect adjustment mechanism in the theoretical system based upon natural law, and the imperfect adjustment mechanism that is likely to prevail in an actual economy. But his followers – the Keynesians – did not demonstrate such a clarity of understanding. They contrived a deterministic system and a predictive science that assumes the attainment of full employment equilibrium in the same period in which government deficit spending initiatives may be undertaken. Data are then collected in a manner that fulfils the equilibrium condition.

The problem comes in the subtlety of Keynes's distinction, and the failure of his deterministic-oriented followers to make explicit his subtlety, and to convey it in their post-Keynes system. The specific origin of the problem appears to be cast in the explanation of the workings of the national income multiplier. On page 122 of *The General Theory*, Keynes distinguished between the instantaneous equilibrium mechanism of what he called 'the logical theory', and the time lag present in an extant economy between a stimulus to the capital goods industries and the ultimate expansion of national output resulting therefrom.

However, in spite of the obvious need, as Keynes stated it, for 'a construction where saving and net investment can diverge from one another', Professor Shackle (1958) points out that Keynes ultimately portrayed 'these two variables as the same thing'. And it is Keynes's latter portrayal that has become ensconced in the Keynesian system. This occurred in the process of his exposition, according to Axel Leijonhufvud, as Keynes shifted from a clarification that the revision of short-term expectations is a gradual and continuous one, to an exposition on the mechanics of the multiplier that came to portray the multiplier as virtually instantaneous in its operation. Leijonhufvud (1968) describes how this came to be: 'consumption spending becomes treated as a function of realized income and employment becomes treated as an immediate function of realized expenditures. In this way he came to refer to the "multiplier" as though it were instantaneous.'

The problem with assuming that employment increases occur in the same period as the government stimulus is that is infers that the multiplier works instantaneously. The assumption is tantamount to invoking Say's Tautology that saving and investment will be equal at their full employment levels in any period we may choose to observe them. Disequilibrium is therefore precluded. By invoking the power of 'the logical theory', the analyst assumes equilibrium to prevail in that period to which his data pertain. Any extant disequilibrium is therefore eradicated from view. And by virtue of this implicit method, saving and investment become portrayed as merely different names for the same homogeneous behaviour.

A MYSTERY VARIABLE

Ultimately, the explanatory value of our inquiry should be revealed in an improved public policy: one which allows society to control the economic environment to benefit the commonweal. Thus far our principle quarry has been to consider method in economics. We have observed the effects of natural law theory upon the development of conventional economic methodology, and we have acknowledged that the contemporary application of that method may obscure important questions about the actual condition of an extant economy. It is the public policy aspect of economic thought to which we now turn. Specifically, we are concerned to explore how an adjustment in method might lead to a change in perspective: to a consideration of different questions, and perhaps to the recommending of different policies and the attainment of different outcomes.

Saving and investment are obviously different activities, even though they become homogenized in the conventional method. Surely, it would be expedient to consider their behavioural definitions in considerable detail. Also, we should want to know that if they differ in disequilibrium, by what manner it is that they diverge. Specifically, if saving exceeds investment during some extant disequilibrium, precisely what is the nature of the economic variable by which saving is greater than investment? How does this variable come into view only during periods of disequilibrium and then fade from our analytical presence when equilibrium is invoked?

DAVID RICARDO

We can learn a great deal about the implications of using comparative static analysis by extrapolating from the economic system developed by David Ricardo. His system can clarify the 'heroic' assumption of continuous equilibrium in an extant economic system, and it can also make visible to us the nature of the mystery disequilibrium variable.

Ricardo, himself, is somewhat enigmatic in the development of economic thought. He was born in 1772, the son of a successful stockbroker who had relocated to London from Holland. The younger Ricardo 'struck out' on his own at a young age, and before the end of his third decade he had amassed a considerable fortune on the London Exchange. With his fortune he acquired land, became a member of the English gentry and sat in the House of Lords. In his quasi-retirement, his pastime became political economy and his interest was in the improvement of the economic condition of his countrymen.

In this capacity Ricardo became the 'systematizer' of the scheme perpetrated by Adam Smith. His analysis and writings were undertaken in the early part of the nineteenth century – contiguous with the birth of the Industrial Revolution. The *Weltanschauung* of Ricardo's system or model was agricultural, pre-industrial, and barter-oriented. It considers the agricultural entrepreneur who rents land and hires labour with the aim of making a profit. Ricardo's entrepreneur produces a single commodity, corn and pays his obligations solely in that medium. So, everyone works for corn, everyone consumes corn, and the unit of exchange is measured in corn. What a convenient system for the simplification of such complex concepts as saving and investment!

There are but two things that the household sector can do with its corn income: corn can either be consumed or it can be saved. Saving is therefore defined as any household income that is not consumed in the current period. In this simple two-sector system all investment is undertaken by businesses, which are agricultural entrepreneurs.

The production of corn at the hand of the capitalist entrepreneur is contrasted with its production in traditional or feudal society. There, output was assumed to be stationary from generation to generation. The lord of the manor, in whose service the serfs were bound, loaned seed corn and land to the peasantry, and received corn as 'rent' at the time of harvest. We shall define rent as the payment to any asset held in fixed supply, such as land. Since production is static, the shares going to the landlord and to the peasantry classes are fixed with time. Output may be expanded only if the resource base – serfs and land – is expanded, or if technology is expanded. As was the case with feudal society, Ricardo assumed the resource and technology base to be invariant in static society.

THE ENTREPRENEUR

Capitalism introduces a novel method for the organization of society's resources in contrast with traditional economic society. In Adam Smith's system – raised to a more elegant level by the systemization of David Ricardo – economic man is no longer portrayed as being bound in feudal servitude. Rather, he acts as a free agent who may competitively trade his labour services in the market place, But this is not the most novel aspect of emergent capitalism. Its principal uniqueness is portrayed in the person of a new entity – the entrepreneur. So in Ricardo's system, three classes rather than two are represented: labourers, who receive wages; landlords, who receive rent; and entrepreneurs who receive profit.

One might assume that the emergence of a third class of economic citizen would draw resources from, and therefore lessen the distributional share going to, the other two. But such is not the case in the ideological vision embodied in capitalist doctrine. The reason is economic growth. The entrepreneur is portrayed as someone very different from the role played by the feudal peasant. Indeed, he contracts for labour with the new labouring class, and he pays rent to the landlord class. But he is also responsible for the management of economic resources that produces a growth in output, rather than a perpetuation of the stationary status quo.

The shares of the landlord and the labouring classes are not lessened. The class of entrepreneurs, then, earns its livelihood by claiming the difference between the stationary output of society, and the ever-larger output that results from capitalist production. Economic growth is the social benefit provided by the entrepreneur, and it is the entrepreneur who receives the value of that social benefit in the form of profit.

But how does Smith – and therefore Ricardo – assume that output can be made larger period after period? The answer lies in capital investment, and in its distinction from traditional saving which also occurs in a static feudal economy. Recall that saving is any act of non-consumption. Saving must be positive for static society to be perpetuated. This is because some capital is inevitably consumed in the production of current output. In the Ricardian system the capital that is consumed is seed corn that is committed to the land in the spring. It is reclaimed from the crop harvest in the autumn and retained for planting in the year following. A stationary, static economy prevails from agricultural year to agricultural year when the quantity of saving is identical to the quantity of investment in seed corn.

ACCUMULATION

We must consider further the act of capitalist investment at spring planting. Risk is inevitably involved, for it is not possible to control for all factors in the environment. Certain risks are implicit in a static, feudal economy. The amount and timing of precipitation, insects or heat may impact crop growth to produce a bountiful harvest, or to produce nothing but famine. In the feudal system there existed certain conventions of charity. For instance, it would be inappropriate according to medieval law for certain peasants to starve while other peasants or the landlord maintained a surplus. In contrast, the capitalist entrepreneur acts to create a surplus. It is his incentive. In doing so he relinquishes his claim to the charity of social convention. By not committing his accumulation to the charity of others, and investing it instead, he risks economic failure and the reality that he has no claim but to the fruits of his own efforts and outcomes.

There are other services that the entrepreneur offers in capitalist society, beyond bearing increased risk in comparison with his feudal peasant counterpart. Principally, these are skill and industry. Skill may be proffered in the form of knowledge or talents that transcend the convention of traditional society. It is also an outcome of vocational specialization that does not exist in feudal society. Industry means that the entrepreneur has a commitment to the endeavour which extends substantially beyond the provision of a set number of hours of labour. Industry is the process whereby the entrepreneur obtains a bountiful outcome by exercising 'stewardship' over the crops. It means that he is solely accountable, and his livelihood hangs in the balance. If something can be done to correct problems as they occur, and to minimize the variance between the actual harvest and the potential harvest, then industry requires him to perform the 'something', whatever it may be.

Carefully note the distinction between saving and investment in the Ricardian system. Saving is nothing more than refraining from the consumption of some portion of current period income. Saving from the current period can be added to the pool of saving from prior periods to form accumulation, or accumulated saving. Simply put, it is a surplus containing past and present saving.

Table 3.1   Quasi-Ricardian taxonomy

Total revenue (Output price × Quantity sold)
(minus) Payment to variable input (labour)
(equals) Quasi-rent
(minus) Cost of borrowed resources
(equals) Gross profit
(minus) Depreciation
(equals) Net profit/Capitalist income
(minus) Capitalist consumption
(equals) Capitalist saving

Investment requires that some portion of accumulation be committed to production with skill, with industry, and in the face of risk. The sum of all accumulation so held is the stock of capital. We differentiate between capital, which is a stock, and investment, which is a flow into the stock of capital. Stated another way, investment is a current activity whereas capital is the stock of present and prior investment activities.

To facilitate the development of our Ricardian taxonomy, let us reiterate the process as it is described in Table 3.1. Total revenue in this simplified system is the unit price of grain multiplied by the number of units produced and sold in the current period. Since gross profit is the difference between total revenue and total cost, we must consider cost in detail. The first cost that is paid is the cost of variable input labour, which is the wage bill. The residual is the payment to the fixed input, which is called quasi-rent. From quasi-rent must be paid the costs of borrowed resources which provide for rentier consumption. If the capitalist has borrowed from himself or others to acquire and retain a fixed asset, then the residual following this payment is gross profit.

From gross profit is subtracted depreciation expenses, leaving a residual of net profit or capitalist income. In Ricardo's crude system, depreciation is the value of the seed corn, sown in the spring, and reclaimed in kind from the autumn harvest. Capitalist income in this simple system is equal to the value of real growth in the economy during the agricultural year. The entrepreneur may dispose of his income as may anyone else. It can either be consumed or saved. If saved, it is added to accumulation. And, it can either be loaned out or invested. If used in the former capacity, the entrepreneur becomes a rentier with regard to that portion of his accumulation. Or it may be invested with skill, industry and in the face of risk, thereby qualifying the holder as a capitalist entrepreneur with that portion of accumulation.

Profit surely benefits the capitalist entrepreneur, directly. But it is assumed to benefit the whole of society, indirectly. Since output is larger, some of the difference may be invested, thereby creating even more output, income and employment.

NON-PRODUCTIVE ASSET USE

Our extrapolation of David Ricardo's system allows us to make an important distinction between what we shall call productive and non-productive asset use. We shall declare an asset to be productive when it is held in capital; that is, when current saving or prior accumulation has been committed to production with skill, industry, and in the face of risk. Growth is the outcome. On the other hand, a non-productively held asset is not committed with skill, industry or risk. It is merely loaned out, as the landlord would loan out land or corn, with limited risk, which is the possibility of payment default. The return to assets so held is economic rent, or interest. Non-productively held resources do not produce a growth outcome. In this scheme they earn rent, which is differentiated from profit.

It is crucial to acknowledge the heroic nature of Say's Tautology as it is portrayed in this simple Ricardian system. To require everything that is saved to also be invested means that no portion of current income is held non-productively. No portion finds its way into rentier use to benefit rentier consumption. Every unit of saving out of capitalist income is committed to investment. Stated more precisely, the quantity of capital in service is increased, from the size of holdings in the last period, by the exact amount of saving. The equilibrium condition requires that entrepreneurs refrain from acting as rentiers with any portion of saving.

DISEQUILIBRIUM

We have acknowledged that saving and investment equality can result in stationary equilibrium if the quantity saved exactly offsets the quantity of capital consumed. In such a system gross investment equals depreciation and therefore net investment is zero. Since there is no growth outcome, there is no profit. Now we must consider the character of economic society in Ricardo's model of capitalism. By imposing the equilibrium condition under conditions of economic growth, it is implicitly assumed that the rate of saving and investment, and therefore the rate of growth, are invariant from period to period. This is called a steady state, and it is differentiated from a stationary state which is the special case of a stationary state with zero growth and zero net investment. The invocation of perpetual equality between saving and investment coupled with some constant amount of depreciation in each period, must produce an economic system in which the rates of growth and profit are constant over time. This is the character of what Keynes called the 'logical theory'.

But consider the possible outcomes in an extant economy if equilibrium is not maintained perpetually, and therefore if saving and investment equality is not continuously realized. Given constant depreciation, and if saving exceeds investment, then the rate of output will be falling towards a new, lower equilibrium. Or, if investment exceeds saving, given that full employment has already been attained, then national output will be constrained by the technical limits of production.

The former case, where saving exceeds investment, is obviously the most interesting from a policy point of view. It is the economic glut. Its most visible manifestation in an extant economy was the Great Depression. As Keynes pointed out, disequilibrium is more likely to be the rule than the exception. Of its two possible manifestations, steady state growth or glut, the economic glut is surely the more feasible outcome.

It is insightful to consider the condition of an extant economy in which the rates of growth and profit are varied from period to period as the result of decisions by capitalist entrepreneurs to hold varying portions of current saving in each period in non-productive use. For instance, if saving is greater than investment, output will be falling from the level attained in the previous period. And if investment exceeds saving in a subsequent period, then the rate of output would be growing in that period. If the economy vacillated between over-investing and underinvesting relative to the full employment level of output, then an interesting pattern would be generated that would be similar to the conventional business cycle. Only when the amplitude of the variances was dampened, falling towards zero, would the economy attain a steady state growth path commensurate with the elimination of the cycle.

Of course, conventional analysis of either the neoclassical or Keynesian varieties is incapable of acknowledging the non-productive use of assets, which is responsible for saving and investment inequality in this scenario. It is precluded as a possibility by virtue of the conventional use of comparative static analysis. It is significant to acknowledge, however, that the equilibrium condition that can be inputed to Ricardo's formal model is not nearly so necessary nor apparent in the work of Adam Smith.

In fact, the distinction between productive and non-productive asset use is present in the *Wealth of Nations*. In Book II, Smith attempted to clarify his position on the nature of wealth. He lived and wrote during a period in which the prevailing economic doctrine was that of the mercantilists. The mercantilists held that wealth was obtained through trade to obtain gold bullion. Doing so was vital to financing the wars of the developing nation states of Europe in the sixteenth, seventeenth and eighteenth centuries.

Smith's position on the nature of wealth differed sharply from that of the mercantilists. To Smith, national wealth – which has come to be called national income – was created through 'the exchangeable value of the annual produce of the land and labour of the country'. Accordingly, 'productive labour' is that which produces a tangible good with market value. Non-productive labour, on the other hand, produces intangibles, such as the services of artisans or professionals. It is this distinction between productive and non-productive labour in the *Wealth of Nations* that is analogous to our distinction in Ricardo between productive and non-productive asset use.

Ekelund and Hebert (1983) point out that Smith's distinction between productive and non-productive labour has been much maligned. Recall that services – particularly professional services – were not marketed in the same competitive way in Adam Smith's day as is in contemporary society. Certainly it is absurd to characterize the service industries as unproductive because they produce no tangible output. Rather, what Smith was driving at was the distinction between those activities that increase net investment, and thus serve the end of economic growth, and those activities that serve merely to enhance the well-being of households. Ekelund and Hebert (1983) emphasize that Smith did not consider workers and industries which he labelled non-productive to be useless; he simply did not regard their activities as furthering the goal of economic growth.

HOARDING

Ricardo's system is useful to the formal definition of investment, saving and accumulation. It also helps us to identify and to define disequilibrium. But because of its embodiment of Newtonian mechanics, it is ultimately incompatible with disequilibrium and therefore the retention of any portion of current saving in non-productive use. We can consider non-productive use, and therefore disequilibrium, in the less formal construction of Adam Smith.

The name we select for the act of retention of some portion of saving in non-productive use, is hoarding. It is descriptive of the withdrawal of gold from circulation for purposes of speculation during the Great Depression. A hoard is a hidden supply or a fund stored up. The term does not have a great deal of meaning in conventional economic literature. To monetarists it is associated with speculation during monetary panics, including the Great Depression. In a gold-backed economy such as the one prevailing in 1933, transactors could be motivated to hold money rather than to hold capital in anticipation of speculative profits from deflation.

Hoarding is also compatible with Keynes's speculative demand for money, although it is not compatible with the Keynesian demand for money as an asset in which the quantity so held is inversely related to he rate of interest. During the Depression individuals were not likely to be motivated to hold gold because its opportunity cost, in comparison with other asset choices, fell with the market rate of interest. Rather, gold was more likely to be held as an alternative to tangible investment and as a hedge against the return to prosperity. As such, hoarding is a non-productive use of saving. It does not represent a backward shift of the saving function in the Keynesian system. Indeed, it should be represented as the difference between saving and investment. It is the amount by which disequilibrium investment falls below its previous equilibrium level.

KEYNESIANISM AND MONETARISM

In Chapter 2 we considered the Keynesian and monetarist explanations of the causes of the Great Depression. Policy prognostications growing out of their respective diagnoses were also considered. Now, having investigated the significance of the conventional method in economic theory, and having described the disequilibrium variable of hoarding, we are prepared to inquire into whether our analytical understanding of the Great Depression is enhanced. Specifically, what are the causes and theoretically suggested cures of glut in a gold-backed economy?

Recall in the Keynesian system that the equilibrium level of national income can be propelled downwards if the endogenous saving function shifts backwards or if the exogenous investment function shifts downwards. We might consider if either one or both of these explanations is compatible with the concept of disequilibrium hoarding.

That the marginal propensity to consume and the marginal propensity to save are constant implies that the consumption and saving functions are stable, and therefore unlikely to shift. What, then, might account for a backward shift in the saving function, according to the Keynesian perspective? According to a popular principles-level textbook by Campbell R. McConnell (1984), there are six possibilities. Without listing them, among the most interesting is a change in household expectations.

We have observed that hoarding of gold was portrayed by what Keynes called the speculative demand for money. Holding gold in a gold-backed economy surely constitutes non-productive use. But instead of constituting a shift in the saving function, it represents a use to which saving is put. When money gold is hoarded it is an alternative to investment, and not an alternative to saving. Consequently, the quantity of investment in some period is reduced by the amount of gold hoarded. Saving therefore exceeds investment by the amount of hoarding occurring during the period.

The obscurity of the speculative demand for money is clarified substantially through viewing the economic tableau in disequilibrium when hoarding is ongoing. But it is typically the saving function which Keynesians shift, and not the investment function, to hypothetically portray money speculation. And, while this has the advantage of not eroding the theoretical constancy of the saving function, it allows one to see the outcome of hoarding, but not its actual occurrence. The outcome of hoarding in a gold-backed economy is a reduction of the quantity of investment by the amount of hoarding. But, while Keynesians are able to argue from their model that an upward shift in the investment function would correct the problem, they are unable to use the model to get at more direct and potentially richer policy solutions.

Similarly, the monetarists correctly perceive of the Depression as an extended panic in which money was withdrawn from circulation, thereby constraining output. Actually, both sides are partially right. The Depression was a monetary phenomenon to the extent that it was extended by the withdrawal of gold from active circulation. But it was also an investment phenomenon, as disequilibrium analysis demonstrates, in that gold hoarding reduced the quantity of current investment, and therefore output.

The policy problem comes from the myopic position taken by the parties to the debate. Neither side acknowledges disequilibrium, and therefore neither side acknowledges hoarding. Rather, each projects into the present a particular aspect of the Depression, either a backward shift in the saving function or a reduction of the money supply. Of course, the respective solutions proposed by these two systems follow from the diagnoses. Unfortunately, neither of these myopic views is likely to explain efficiently a changing and imperfect world in which extant disequilibrium is likely to be the rule, and in which the very nature of money has changed dramatically. Since money is no longer backed by gold, there is no longer incentive to hoard it as an alternative to holding investment. In a fiat money economy other objects are preferred instead, such as real estate, antiques, or other objects which we shall discuss in Part IV.

RETRACKING THE PARADIGM

At this juncture it is instructive to summarize our theoretical quest. What we observe is a common paradigm which has its basis in eighteenth-century natural law theory, and which dictates the methodological convention of three economic systems based upon it. The first is the neoclassical system. It fully embodies all the aspects of the classical world view, and fails to distinguish between an extant economy and the timeless and frictionless character of the perfect order portrayed by natural law.

The second is the Keynesian system which acknowledges the

methodological constraint. However, like the neoclassical system, it limits itself to viewing an extant economy only in equilibrium. As a consequence, it is only able to observe the outcome of economic dysfunction, which is a reduced level of investment and a reduced quantity of output. The system prescribes a role for government which is absent in the doctrinaire neoclassical formulation. It becomes the responsibility of government to correct for *ex ante* disequilibrium by insuring that the aggregate level of investment and therefore the aggregate level of spending is held at its full employment level. The public policy manifestation of the Keynesian revolution is therefore revealed in a new presence for the government in economic matters, beginning in 1933.

The third intellectual system, monetarism, is also limited by the methodological convention that precludes time in economics. Its focus, of course, is myopically upon the relationship between the money stock and the level of output and prices. It is a crucial relationship. But by failing to capture the significance of disequilibrium as it relates to the primal paradigm, monetarists are unable to connect the relationship of money in an economic system to the significance of other economic variables.

Finally, we summarize the disequilibrium view which also has its roots in the conventional paradigm. However, since it admits time, it permits disequilibria in extant economies to be viewed. Disequilibrium is commensurate with hoarding, which is the holding of assets in non-productive use. Consequently, the policy prescription flowing out of disequilibrium analysis is that government must not only move to set the levels of investment and aggregate spending at their full employment levels, but it must act to create direct disincentives to hoarding. As such, disequilibrium analysis does not divorce itself from the power and continuity of the comparative static method embodied in the conventional paradigm. Rather, it qualifies its applicability to extant economies that are not likely to fulfil the equilibrium condition. Consequently, disequilibrium analysis allows the full power of analysis to proceed, using the conventional method. But in so doing it qualifies the outcomes, and therefore specifies the limits of their applicability in extant economic situations.

Part III

The Economic Milieu

John Maynard Keynes attempted to overcome the limitations of equilibrium analysis in economic theory. But his efforts were only partly successful. Economists who came after him attempted to adapt his ideas to a deterministic and predictive science. The nuance of Keynes's analysis became subverted by a powerful mathematical system which masks the subtle influences of eighteenth-century natural law theory.

Keynesian economics worked quite well until the Vietnam War. A number of economic changes occurred in the five-year period between 1968 and 1973. Among them was the final repudiation of gold as a backing for the international monetary system, and the upsurge of inflation in the United States. Chapter 4, 'Why Keynesian Stabilization Policy Doesn't Work', asserts that inflation in the 1970s caused disequilibrium hoarding. Economic transactors became motivated to shift their wealth positions from productively held assets such as capital, to non-productive assets such as real estate. The resulting reorganization in the structure of the economy resulted in substantial productivity declines.

However, inflation-induced hoarding is not the only problem with the American economy. Since about 1980, America has experienced another problem that has also contributed substantially to productivity decline. It is also related to a glitch in conventional theory. Chapter 5 discusses unexplained problems in the American economy in the mid-1980s. These are principally related to popular organizational strategies such as 'cutback management', corporate raids, or performance budgeting.

4 Why Keynesian Stabilization Policy Doesn't Work?

The mechanics of Keynes's disequilibrium analysis were not highly visible. Rather, these were smuggled into his system by distinguishing between realized and notional quantities of saving and investment. Whereas realized or *ex post* saving and investment are continuously in equality (because an extant economic system can only be viewed in equilibrium), the values of notional or *ex ante* saving and investment are allowed to be unequal.

To illustrate, we begin from a position of *ex post* equilibrium, but with divergent plans for saving and investment in the next period by households and firms. If planned or *ex ante* saving exceeds *ex ante* investment for that prospective period, then the economy can be predicted to reach its next moment of equilibrium at a smaller quantity of output and national income than was obtained at the last equilibrium.

It should be noted that *ex ante* equality between saving and investment is only relevant for a specified length of time in the future. For instance, viewed from the present, notional saving and investment may be equal for a twelve-month interval in the future, unequal for a twenty-four-month interval, but equal for a thirty-six-month period. If notional equality (or inequality) is predicted, a particular time segment must be specified to which that equality pertains.

However, since *ex post* equality between saving and investment is a requirement of conventional analysis, time is ultimately disregarded, even in Keynes's system. Consequently, equilibrium is 'invoked' coterminus with the ending of any real time period for which inquiry may be initiated. The professional convention is to declare the analytical lens to be in focus at annual intervals contiguous with the government accounting cycle, or fiscal year. But this is an arbitrary specification that does not necessarily coincide with extant equality between saving and investment. Even so, economic data may be collected so as to treat saving and investment as essentially the same, and therefore to make no apparent distinction between the two.

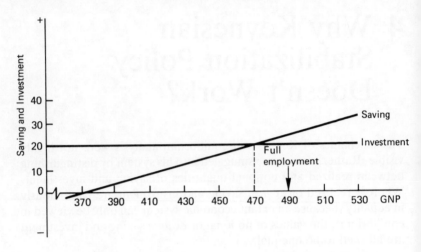

Figure 4.1   Equilibrium at less than full employment

Everything that is withheld from consumption is considered to be invested.

It is possible, then, that an actual economy could be in *ex post* disequilibrium on a given date – such as 31 December – when the annual accounts of government may be closed, but it would be concealed by the conventional method of analysis. For, by ending one accounting period and beginning another, equilibrium is contrived. Data are collected so as to confirm this postulate. The economic analyst lacks any means of conducting an *ex post* analysis in any other presumed state but equilibrium.

Our specific concern focuses upon the outcome of a Keynesian policy to stimulate the economy to full employment equilibrium. The graphical mechanics of such a stimulus are illustrated in Figure 4.1. Saving is equal to investment at 470 units of national income. But this is not the full employment level. Analysts determine that another twenty units of national income per year must be created to provide full employment.[1]

Investment is exogenous in this model. It is determined by business expectations of profitability. In this illustration the twenty units of business investment, *ex ante*, is less than the twenty-five units of household saving that would be forthcoming at full employment (see Table 4.1). Hence, the 490 level is not sustainable because saving would exceed investment at that level, and disequilibrium would prevail with increasing unemployment and decreasing output and

Table 4.1   Determination of equilibrium level of gross national product

GNP	Saving	Investment	Tendency of employment, output and income
370	−5	20	Increasing
390	0	20	Increasing
410	5	20	Increasing
430	10	20	Increasing
450	15	20	Increasing
470	20	20	Equilibrium
490	25	20	Decreasing
510	30	20	Decreasing
530	35	20	Decreasing

national income, until a national income level of 470 units is obtained. This is the only level of national income compatible with twenty units of investment.

Since households are predisposed to save more than businesses are predisposed to invest at full employment, and therefore since that level of national income is not sustainable, stimulation of business investment would appear expedient. Perhaps the business community could be motivated to place an additional five units of investment at every level of national income. This is unlikely, however, since business investment is motivated by expectations of profitability. Increased private investment is not likely to coincide with depressed expectations.

Keynes's prescription was for government to intervene and to provide the 'investment shortfall' that the business community is unable to generate. Note in this illustration that Keynesian analysis prescribes the government to inject five únits of investment. The outcome is twenty new units of national income, which propels this hypothetical system to its full employment level. Government must inject only the amount of the investment shortfall, or five units, and not the entire amount of the national income shortfall, which is twenty units.

This relationship between the government stimulus and the expansionary impact upon national income is called the national income multiplier. It is calculated as one over the marginal propensity to save (MPS). Since the MPS in this example is 1/4, the multiplier is equal to 1 divided 1/4, or 4. The Keynesian expectation is that the government injection of five units of investment will result in the creation of twenty new units of national income. The government stimulus is efficient because for every one dollar of investment that is injected in this example, four new dollars of national income are created.

Now, we want to focus upon the possibility that the national income multiplier could grow smaller with each successive use. If this is so, government would be required to inject an increasing stimulus in each successive period in which *ex ante* saving exceeded *ex ante* investment. Economists describe the national income multiplier as actually operating in the range between 2 and 2.5. However, there is evidence that the multiplier has been declining in recent years. In a survey of the experience of major European countries, Richard Cooper (1984) points out that the multiplier has declined by anywhere from 12 to 60 per cent since the 1960s. Cooper believes that similar declines have occurred in the United States.

What may explain this decline? An appeal to the disequilibrium hoarding hypothesis is revealing. Our particular policy focus is the 1970s in which inflation was rampant, and transactors were sheltering their wealth from currency depreciation by holding inelastically supplied goods. Real estate, objects d'art, metallic coins, stamps, antiques and vintage cars were among the favourite placements.

The basic Keynesian system, so popular in economic policy circles in the 1960s and 1970s, does not account for hoarding behaviour. We shall carefully consider the ramifications of this omission. Suppose that economic analysts estimate the MPS to be 1/4, and therefore the multiplier to be four. Since twenty additional units of national income are desired to reach full employment, the policy prescription is clear. *Ex ante* saving exceeds *ex ante* investment at the full employment level of national income, and an expected shortfall of twenty units of national income in the next period can be overcome by a government injection of five units in that period.

But suppose, because of inflation, that transactors decide to invest only one half of the portion of the government stimulus that is saved, and to hoard the other half as a hedge against inflation. If this is so, then the full employment level of business investment and government spending will not be forthcoming. The outcome will be an investment and national income shortfall. Some progress will have been made towards obtaining full employment, but it will appear that the government stimulus was less efficient than expected, perhaps because the multiplier was overestimated.

The outcome is illustrated in Figure 4.2. Note that rather than the

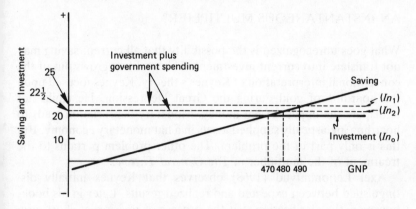

Figure 4.2   Government stimulus of five units increases investment by only 2 1/2 units

five-unit injection producing twenty units of national income, that it produces only ten units instead. The intent of the managers of the economy is to shift from In_0 to In_1, but the investment outcome becomes In_2. In this case combined business investment and government spending has reached only 22 1/2 – 2 1/2 units short of the full employment equilibrium quantity. The balance of 2 1/2 units that should have become investment, ended up being hoarded in inelastically supplied objects, instead.[2]

But economic analysts are likely to interpret the shortfall as their error to calculate the multiplier correctly, and therefore to calculate the MPS. In reality, however, the failure is an outcome of the inability of the conventional theory to account for disequilibrium hoarding, which has taken the form of inflation-induced placements in non-productive assets. So a second round of stimuli ensues. Now, using an adjusted multiplier of two rather than four, the managers of the economy inject another five units of government stimulus, in hopes of gaining the full employment target of ten additional units, or 490 units. But again, since disequilibrium hoarding is not taken into account, all the increment of saving that is forthcoming at the higher level of government-stimulated income is not transmitted into investment. An increasing portion of new saving becomes hoarded. Policy assessments in subsequent periods perceive the multiplier to be decreasing. Keynesian policies are thereby revealed to be of decreasing effectiveness, and inching towards the goal of full employment is gained only by incurring astronomically increasing social costs.

AN INSTANTANEOUS MULTIPLIER?

What goes unrecognized is the possibility that all current saving may not translate into current investment. This problem grows out of the conventional interpretation of Keynes's theory. Keynes focused upon the hoarding of gold during the Great Depression. He could not anticipate the impact of fiat money. Monetary depreciation leads to hoarding inelastically supplied assets in a fiat monetary economy. But this is only part of the problem. The other problem pertains to the treatment of the multiplier in *The General Theory*.

Axel Leijonhufvud (1968) observes that Keynes initially distinguished between expected and realized results. Later in his book, however, the clarification that the process of revision of short-term expectations is a gradual and continuous one became virtually absent. Consumption spending became treated as a virtually immediate function of realized income. In this way, Keynes came to refer to the multiplier as though it was instantaneous. The theoretical manifestation of this obscure problem became the treatment of saving and investment as being equal, *ex post*, in every period. If Keynes understood that extant economies do not adjust so instantaneously, he failed to clarify the implications of *ex post* disequilibrium in his reconciliation with neoclassical theory.

G.L.S. Shackle (1958) refers to Keynes's omission of an explicit theoretical clarification of why *ex post* disequilibrium could not exist 'as one more illustration of the unconscious application to economics of ideas derived from classical physical dynamics'. In spite of his intuitive observation that the theory must be modified to allow saving and investment to diverge from one another, he portrayed these two variables as 'two names for the same thing'. After Keynes's death in 1946, his followers created a predictive and deterministic system upon his rather abstract summary. The 'Hicks–Hansen' formulation of Keynes's thought perpetuates the homogenization of saving and investment behaviour by forcing them to continuous equality, in conformity with the methodological convention.

NATURAL RATE OF UNEMPLOYMENT

The connection between inflation and hoarding is becoming increasingly clear. For Keynesian stimuli to work effectively, they must be accompanied by accommodative monetary policy. In an economy

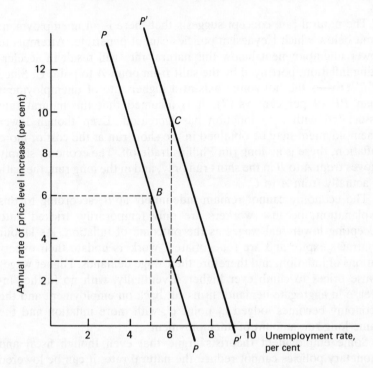

Figure 4.3 The Phillips curve shows an apparent trade-off between inflation and unemployment

with fiat money, government abuse of its money-creating powers is likely. It is the reality of too many dollars chasing too few goods, with inflation becoming more severe over time, that motivates transactors to improve their positions through hoarding inelastically supplied goods.

In the 1970s, the Phillips curve was a popular device for attempting to explain the alleged public trade-off between inflation and unemployment. In the short run, so the explanation went, lower unemployment could be 'bought' at the cost of higher inflation. Congress could pursue Keynesian policies designed to reduce unemployment, but only by incurring more inflation. But the attractiveness of the trade-off wained in the 1960s and 1970s with evidence that the Phillips curve was shifting outwards, over time, from *PP* to *P'P'* in Figure 4.3. The natural rate of unemployment hypothesis emerged to explain this phenomenon.

The natural rate concept suggests that there is an unemployment limit below which Keynesian policies cannot penetrate. Attempts to lower unemployment below this natural rate will result in accelerating inflation, portrayed by the shift from point A to point C. Since $P'P'$ crosses the horizontal axis at a higher rate of unemployment than PP (9 per cent vs. 7), it is assumed that the natural rate associated with zero inflation has increased. Even though lower unemployment may be obtained in the short run at the cost of more inflation, there is no long run Phillips trade-off. The economy simply moves from A to B in the short run only, and in the long run, the path is actually from A to C.

The economy cannot remain indefinitely at B, according to this explanation, because workers are only temporarily 'tricked' into accepting lower real wages as the outcome of inflation. As labour contracts expire and are renegotiated, workers update their expectations of inflation, and therefore their wage demands. Higher wages cause prices to climb ever higher. Eventually, with no further increase in aggregate demand, firms cut back on employment and the economy becomes lodged at point C, with more inflation and the same long-run amount of unemployment.

Some employment theorists argue that even though fiscal and monetary policies cannot reduce the natural rate, it can be lowered through microeconomic policies which impact structural unemployment. These include the correction of skill mismatches, location mismatches, institutional barriers, imperfect information flows and transfer payment discrepancies. According to this view, the Phillips curve trade-off during the 1980s has become more attractive, falling from $P'P'$ towards PP, because of improvements in labour force utilization.

But even though the Phillips relationship has been improving under supply-side policies, there is no evidence that the productive utilization of the labour force has dramatically improved. Instead, the significant difference between the 1970s and the 1980s is the rate of inflation. How could a reduction in the rate of inflation possibly cause an improvement in the Phillips relationship? The disequilibrium hypothesis provides an alternative explanation to the natural rate explanation that leftward shifts in the curve are principally caused by improvements in labour productivity.

Inflation-induced hoarding causes transactors to divert an increasing portion of new saving into hoarding, rather than into investment. The ratio of investment to national income therefore declines. Accommodative monetary policy continues to accelerate the engines of inflation, exacerbating the problem. Since a capital shortfall exists, productivity lags. Hoarding behaviour encourages all society's assets, including its labour force, to be less efficiently utilized. On the other hand, a decline in the rate of inflation, which has occurred in the first half of this decade, decreases the incentive to hoard assets inelastically supplied.

The retention of a decreasing portion of society's assets in non-productive use leads to improved productivity and growth. These are the outcomes which appear to shift the Phillips curve to the left. In reality, the trade-off between inflation and unemployment is illusory. Both variables are related to a third one, which is undefined by conventional theory. It is the inflation-induced retention of assets in non-productive use.

Counter-Keynesian policies to improve the economy are likely to focus upon reducing inflation and improving labour market efficiency. But rather than concentrating directly upon the labour market, an effective policy to mitigate the effects of inflation should focus upon hoarding behaviour instead. Hoarding should be curtailed as an object of public policy, or the income benefits that accrue to hoarding behaviour should be taxed away.

Without any significant shift away from Keynesian, monetarist or supply-side variations on the prevailing paradigm, which has been the conventional wisdom since the Great Depression, we are likely to see a vacillation in economic policies. From Keynesian policies which stimulate short-term employment gains at the expense of long-term inflation, we are likely to swing towards supply-oriented policies which emphasize productivity and monetary constraint. But neither of these isolated positions will deliver economic improvement. Neither system allows for disequilibrium, and hoarding is therefore precluded. In frustration, then, we might expect the political pendulum to swing back and forth between these two extreme positions, while all the time the economic vitality of the country is depleted and the American public becomes increasingly sceptical.

5 Unexplained Problems

Americans wanted to believe that the supply-oriented proposals of the Reagan administration were better alternatives than the failed demand-oriented Keynesian policies of the Johnson, Nixon, Ford and Carter administrations. But the supply-side prescription for economic success has created many unexplained consequences for the American public, and these do not appear to be compatible with the success claims being made by Reaganomics advocates.

Productivity improvement is the principle source of economic improvement. It is highly correlated with the quantity of investment. Investment policies were proposed by supply-siders which encouraged saving through lucrative tax breaks to the wealthy, and which provided an accelerated cost recovery system of depreciation allowances to American corporations. However, in spite of these touted schemes for stimulating productivity, the American public has been continuously bombarded by reports of financial manipulation which suggest that productivity considerations are being neglected, or even impeded.

A popular perception is that it is the corporate financiers, and not the managers of production, that are manipulating American businesses and reaping enormous wealth benefits therefrom. An article from the 7 April 1984 issue of *The Economist* describes some of the fortunes that have been made by corporate raiders. Rupert Murdoch, for instance, made nearly $50 million by selling back a 7 per cent stake in Warner Communications at a 42 per cent premium; James Goldsmith and other investors made a $50 million profit by buying and selling back an 8.6 per cent share of the St Regis paper company, and Texas oilman T. Boone Pickens and other private investors are estimated to have made over $700 million from Socal Oil's victory in the auction of Gulf Oil.

MERGER-MANIA

Irwin L. Kellner (1987), chief economist for Manufacturers Hanover, describes the contemporary corporate milieu:

> Streamline. Restructure. Become lean and mean. Reorganize. Spin off. Buy back. Merge or acquire. These and other words are being

used to describe what amounts to the greatest overhauling of corporate America in the postwar era. Many of today's top companies look very different than they did just a few short years ago. Some corporations have gotten bigger by buying others, while other companies have become smaller by selling some of their divisions.

Proponents of corporate acquisitions argue that the separation of ownership and control in modern publicly-held companies has predisposed managers to act in their own self-interest, rather than to advocate for stockholders. But often the tactics that are used allegedly to increase shareholder equity are questionable. Specifically, there is the development that has come to be known as 'greenmail'. This is the ransoming by a company of its stock from the clutches of a raider who has bought some shares and has threatened to buy enough to take it over. As hostile takeovers become more common, companies are using new defences such as 'poison pill' or 'scorched earth'. These plunge a company so deeply into debt that a takeover would bankrupt the raider.

High interest costs associated with greater corporate debt levels mean that resources must be diverted from such other uses as research and development, job creation and capital investment. Interest paid as a percentage of pretax profits has been about 50 per cent in recent years. This compares with less than 25 per cent in the 1970s, and around 10 per cent in the 1960s. The short-term pressure required to meet the immediacy imposed by the debt is akin to forcing managers to operate within a straitjacket. Immediate profits are generated for the raiders, but often at the expense of thoughtful and orderly long-term corporate development. Defences that corporations must erect to maintain their independence wind up costing jobs as divisions are spun off and staffs are pared. In addition, the quality of much corporate debt deteriorates with the proliferation of risky 'junk bonds' to finance the capers.

In the typical acquisition there is no reason to believe that the acquiring company will manage the assets better than the raided one. The acquirer simply thinks that the stock market is undervaluing the worth of the target company's assets. Takeover and reorganisation or liquidation are an easy source of speculative profits for the raiders.

Economist Lester Thurow (1985) describes how excessive corporate acquisitions produce short-term planning horizons for American corporations. Raiding occurs in an environment in which everyone responds rationally to individual incentives, but the sum total of those rational choices adds up to 'social stupidity'. Unfortunately, the American tax system, particularly spurred by the Economic Recovery Tax Act of 1981 (ERTA), compounded merger-mania prior to tax reform in 1986. The accelerated cost recovery system of depreciation allowances provided many companies with tax credits which could not be used directly, since their allowable deductions for depreciation were larger in some cases than their current profits. With the abolishment of lease-backs or safe-harbour leasing (buying and selling of tax credits) in 1982, firms were often left with mergers as the only vehicle for using the tax credits.

RATE OF RETURN ANALYSIS

Private firms are not the only ones that supplant production with a myopic focus upon finance. The shift to finance-oriented management styles also occurs in government, and in non-profit organizations such as universities and hospitals. Its manifestation is not like the raiding that occurs in the private sector, but the behavioural outcomes are essentially similar. Finance-oriented decisions are very different from production-oriented ones. The shift to finance is also accompanied by a change in management and leadership practices and strategies. Portfolio management theory suggests to businesses and to public and non-profit organizations alike that rate of return analysis and performance budgeting are synonymous with effective management. Unfortunately, long-term outcomes may be deleterious to the ability of organizations to contribute to the commonweal.

As an illustration, consider the use of rate of return analysis by a hypothetical university. Its president may seek to expand his sphere of influence by increasing his control over the annual budget process. For instance, a systematic programme of forced austerity over three or four years may wring out any 'fat' that may exist in the budgets of academic deans. Forcing each college or school to cut a certain percentage from its previous year's budget is a useful way to identify any capacity that is not immediately related to the institutional goal as perceived by the president.

When annual percentage cuts can no longer be tolerated by a particular dean without causing obvious harm to essential programmes, then the dean is forced to defend those programmes with voluminous data. The procedure is generally known as zero-based budgeting. It ties programme output directly to budget. To the extent that the president's sense may be better than the dean's of what a particular programme ought to be doing, then the outcome may be favourable. But since the president stands further from the programme than does the dean, he or she may take restrictive or reallocative budget decisions which are expedient in the short run, but that may be ill-advised in the long run.

The 'worst-case' scenario of performance budgeting is the case in which a profitable programme may actually become the victim of this 'management-through-the-budget' strategy. Efforts to use scarce organizational resources more efficiently by the president may result in reallocations from one school or college to another. The assumption, of course, is that the expanding school can use the marginal budget more efficiently than the contracting one. It is likely that rate of return analysis will be used to determine the efficiency with which increased or reduced levels of budget will be utilized. From the president's perspective, the opportunity cost of allowing a marginal dollar to remain with college A, is the possibly higher rate of return that it might obtain by being shifted to school B, instead.

PERFORMANCE BUDGETING

To make this illustration more explicit, we shall assume that the president announces to his deans that his strategy for making his university more efficient is to raise the rate of return on the annual budgeted expenses of each of its schools and colleges. Annual budget proposals will be scrutinized to encourage the highest rate of return possible for each school or college. Each is treated as a profit centre, with tuition revenues computed on one hand, and expenses for faculty and staff salaries, duplicating, office equipment, etc., on the other. The difference between revenues of the profit centre and direct expenses is not profit, since the university does not exist to earn a profit. Rather, it is the contribution – called 'indirect' – which the school or college makes to the operation of non-revenue-earning units of the service-oriented university. In a university, indirect pays the expenses of the library, maintaining buildings and grounds, and so forth.

The president probably begins with some expectation of minimum performance on the part of each of his schools. Let's assume, for convenience, that a rate of return of 2.0 is deemed by the president to

be minimally acceptable, and that higher rates of return are desir-
able. For each profit centre, then, the rate of return is calculated by
dividing tuition revenue by direct budgeted expenses associated with
profit centre operation. An index of 2.0 would indicate that for each
dollar spent directly by a profit centre, another dollar is contributed
to the administration to pay the 'indirect' expenses of the service
units mentioned above.

The worst-case scenario using rate of return analysis could occur if
a profitable programme of a profit centre is reduced, or even terminated, to meet the president's budget guidelines. For example, suppose that a particular college is operating with a revenue-to-cost ratio
below 2.0. To meet the president's mandate in the next budget cycle,
it must either increase its revenues, or reduce its costs, or some
combination of both.

If the mandate (to move the profit centre from below 2.0 to 2.0) is
obtained entirely through new revenue expansion – by adding new
programmes – more than two dollars of new revenue must be earned
for every dollar of cost supporting the new programmes. But this is
heroic since the rate of return on start-up programmes is likely to be
lower than the rate of return on established ones. So the likelihood of
raising the rate of return on a profit centre's budget by adding new
programmes is remote.

Cost reduction is more likely to be attractive than revenue expansion to obtain the president's rate of return mandate. If the profit
centre's existing rate of return (ROR) is below 2.0, then for every
dollar that is cut from one of the school's low-performing programmes, somewhat less than one dollar is lost from its contribution
to administrative indirect. Both the size of the profit centre budget
and its contribution to university indirect are falling, but the rate of
return is rising. In other words, cost-cutting increases the actual rate
of return because costs are declining at a faster rate than the rate at
which revenues are declining. So, a low ROR profit centre would
generally be better advised to reduce its costs rather than to add new
programmes to improve this measure of alleged efficiency.

The worst-case scenario, then, is to cut a budding programme
within the cost centre because its ROR is not yet meeting the
president's goal. This may be an expedient way for the president to
deliver an acceptably low budget to his trustees, but it trades the
long-term well-being of the institution and its programmes for short-
term expediency. If potentially profitable programmes are cut in their
infancy – before they can mature into profitable ones – then the

university is forcing itself to place increasing emphasis upon the current programme menu. In doing so it becomes less resilient and less able to respond to the characteristics of a dynamic future market. Rather than nurturing new product lines, it sacrifices them to a management strategy that is sensitive only to today. It is not sensitive to current sacrifices to gain improved or dynamic products for the future.

Among the problems endemic to this management style based upon ROR analysis is that it assumes that future organizational outcomes are known in the present. It tends to compact the planning horizon of the organization, and to assume that it can respond instantaneously in the future to create new programmes and products to meet changing demand. But the process of developing programmes and products is often an organic one. It requires both nurturing and time. Perhaps the process is even a little mystical: we cannot see perfectly into the future and therefore we are always a little surprised by it when we arrive there.

To the extent that performance budgeting assumes that the future is a logical extension of the past or present, then it is likely that an organization leader will fail to perceive the nuance involved in nurturing present low performers in order to develop them into future high performers. If the budget process cuts away excess capacity – taking muscle along with fat – until only the minimal superstructure is standing, it is also likely to be cutting creativity, initiative and experience. These may be an organization's most precious assets in adapting to the future.

AGRICULTURE

Nowhere is the dichotomy between production and finance more evident than in agriculture. It is characterized by booms and busts, in part because of the independent, competitive nature of the industry with tens of thousands of family farms. Agricultural surpluses do not necessarily decree that the land is being used productively and in the best interest of future generations. Finance-oriented practices may change the structure of the industry, or the quality of the soil, in ways that may effect the industry for many generations to come.

Farmers and ranchers throughout the United States underwent far more financial stress than normal in 1984, and again in 1985. Congress passed a farm bill in December 1985, reflecting efforts to stabilize the incomes of farmers while allowing market forces to influence resource allocation decisions to a greater extent. Net farm income declined 22 per cent between 1984 and 1985, to a substantially lower level than in the 1970s. Farm liquidations because of bankruptcy occurred two to three times greater than normal during 1985. And analysts report that land values have declined by 40 per cent or more from the market peak year of 1981. The US Department of Agricultures estimates that one-fifth of all farms with annual sales of over $40 000 began 1985 in serious financial stress. In addition, 54 000 fell into the category of severely stressed, meaning that debt-asset ratios are greater than 70 per cent, and they have negative cash flows. Among the outcomes of this stress is a haemorrhaging of the farm credit system, and a consolidation of land-holdings into 'stronger hands'.[1]

The essential problem underlying current instability in America's agricultural industry is long-term sustainability. As agricultural analyst Marty Strange (1984) points out, to be sustainable, agriculture must also sustain the people who are a part of it. At present, agriculture ruins a substantial number of lives each year. Financial ruin is obvious. But farming depletes people in other important ways, as evidenced by growing concern about emotional stress among farmers and farm families. The objective of sustainable agriculture, as Marty Strange puts it, should be 'to nourish a renewable pool of human land stewards who earn a healthy living by farming well'.

Astonishingly high crop yields were often reported on the American frontier with the clearing of forests and grasslands. Hans Jenny (1984), an advocate of appropriate agriculture, describes how far-sighted experiments conducted by agricultural universities analyzed the virgin soils and kept track of the changes occurring under different systems of farming. Parcels receiving no fertilizer experienced a rapid decline in the soil's content of organic matter during the early decades, and a slower decline thereafter. Naturally, crop yields diminished.

Jenny argues that America's tradition of manipulating its natural resources for private gain, compounded with short-range policies, has been disastrous for the soil. Further, soil 'malpractice' is rising rather than declining. Since we cannot foresee the needs of America generations from now, Americans must come to acknowledge that those needs will be satisfied by the food that will be grown on the soils that are a legacy of this generation. N.A. Berg (1981), a former chief of the Soil Conservation Service, warns, 'There is no national policy for the United States that places value on the soil resource or on conserving the soil resource.' Moreover, no such policy is in sight.

American agriculture has increasingly emphasized the conventional wisdom of financially motivated organizations. As Strange (1984) points out:

> Farms have become more specialized, relying on the prescriptive application of standard technologies, producing on a large-volume basis, using sophisticated machinery that limits the farmer's ability to adapt or change. Farms increasingly rely on debt to foster expansion. Most important, as competition for land among expanding farms increases land values, the tendency is to separate farm ownership from farm operation.

Jenny and others recommend a complete reappraisal of American farming practices that has its basis in soil conservation – that soil fertility and long-term environmental compatibility come first. The conservation of America's agricultural resources – its soils and its people – can only occur if farms are family rather than corporation-centred, owner operated and internally financed.

Corporate acquisitions, rate of return analysis, and the depletion of American agriculture are limited examples of a plethora of finance-oriented practices that dominate contemporary America. The experts may not acknowledge it, but one need only read the newspapers to recognize that something is seriously wrong with America's productive apparatus.

Part IV

A Second Glitch

The second glitch of economic theory is the profit lacuna. There is no theory that specifies what the rate of profit should be in the neoclassical system. Households and businesses that optimize according to the dictates of the conventional model are likely to undercompensate capital. This may lead to capital shortage, to productivity decline, and therefore to a levelling or a decline in the standard of living.

Chapter 6, 'Asset Conservation', considers the relationship between Marshallian short-period analysis, the staple of undergraduate instruction, and economic growth. The latter occurs when firms maximize total profit by setting output and employment at their theoretically prescribed rates. But the second glitch of economic theory may confuse what these optimal levels should be. The outcome may be an underutilization of capital by the typical firm, and by all firms in society.

The profit lacuna is the subject of Chapter 7. It explains the enigma of neoclassical theory that fails to prescribe what the rate of profit should be. This failure leads to a blurring of the distinction between profit and interest, and therefore between capital and finance. Chapter 8 considers the likely outcome, which is zero sum society. It provides a scenario of how economic progress may cease when the dicta of the neoclassical theory are adopted as the conventional wisdom. In the contemporary milieu, firms adhering to the conventional wisdom are likely to engage in 'money games' such as corporate take-overs, rather than to concentrate their energies on production management.

6 Asset Conservation

Our quest in Part IV is to consider a second glitch in doctrinaire *laissez-faire* capitalism. Since a glitch is a malfunction, our concern is to observe aspects of the conventional economic theory that may explain economic dysfunction, and to set forth a corrective programme to restore traditional capitalist economies to health. Recall that the first glitch of economic theory is unemployment. It results from the disparity between the ideal conditions of the economic archetype which has its basis in natural law, and conditions prevailing in an extant economy. Time and friction are characteristics of an actual economy. When time is present, disequilibrium is the normal outcome. During the gold-backed monetary system of the Great Depression, disequilibrium was revealed in the hoarding of gold in anticipation of its appreciation. The outcome was a shortfall in output, and therefore unemployment resulted.

In Figure 2.7, unemployment is portrayed as a point inside the production possibilities frontier. The efficient utilization of labour and other resources can boost society to its frontier, wherein it can produce the requisite quantity of one or both goods compatible with full employment. Here we see a disparity between Adam Smith's unbounded faith in the unseen hand, and economic reality as it prevailed during the Great Depression. According to Smith, *laissez-faire* works in such a way that the individualistic pursuit of utility will result in an outcome benefiting the commonweal. But through our analysis of the Depression we have observed a tragedy of the commons associated with hoarding gold. Profiting in gold speculation is an illustration of an outcome that may benefit particular individuals, but may not benefit the commonweal. It flies in the face of Adam Smith's unbounded faith in the social welfare-maximizing characteristics of *laissez-faire*.

The commons in medieval society was the community domain which was literally held 'in common'. One thinks, for instance of the Boston Commons, which has become a park in the contemporary era. In feudal society, as today, the commons was not to be appropriated by acts of individualism. If a single peasant violated convention and allowed his cow to graze on its comparatively lush grasses, the outcome was a fat cow which directly benefited the errant peasant. Perhaps violation by one or even a few peasants would not cause community hardship. But if all peasants violated the convention and allowed their cows grazing privileges, the commons' grasses would soon become depleted and the peasantry would ultimately be worse off due to the loss of the community asset. In the fallacy of the commons, an act of individual sovereignty may benefit one, but when it becomes the convention, the community reaps a negative benefit.

We are at present witnessing the unfolding of a second economic tragedy of the commons. Its manifestation is not unemployment, as in the first theoretical glitch, but it is the failure to grow economically, or to create wealth. It is represented in the production possibilities frontier by the failure of the frontier to move outwards with the passage of time. Such is the case with stationary society. Like the fallacy of saving in the first glitch, the fallacy of wealth creation is anomalous with the vision of Adam Smith. We shall explore in detail the utility maximizing, wealth-creating dicta flowing out of that vision. When applied at the level of the individual, substantial material progress may result. But when it becomes commonly accepted as the standard of best practice, the outcome of everyone behaving in like manner may be one which does not benefit the commonweal. The wealth of society may not increase. In fact, it may remain stationary – with zero net investment – or it may even decline.

Surely the attainment of zero growth in an extant economy modelled after the *laissez-faire* archetype is fraught with considerable intellectual problems. Remember that the rationale for the existence of the capitalist class is to create new investment, and therefore wealth and growth. The capitalists' reward – profit – benefits society because as capitalist consumption expands, capitalist demand creates opportunities for other classes to increase their consumption. The living standard is assumed to increase Pareto-optimally, benefiting some or all, without hurting any.

However, when there is no growth, there is no wealth creation, and therefore there is no intellectual justification for private capital ownership. In the stationary state the hypothetical capitalist acts not as a capitalist but as a rentier. His reward is economic rent in return for loaning assets. He merely plays a role in economic society analogous to the role of the landlord in feudal society. His consumption does not benefit others. Rather, if he earns more, it must come from others simultaneously earning less. The only doctrinaire justification in *laissez-faire* for the private ownership of assets in stationary society is that the ownership pattern perpetuates the status quo.

THE MARSHALLIAN SHORT PERIOD

To get at the second glitch of doctrinaire capitalism we must begin by reconsidering briefly the conditions under which growth, investment and profit, and therefore wealth creation, occur in the conventional theory. To do so we begin with the theory of the short period as it was promulgated by Alfred Marshall, the so-called champion of neoclassical economics. His analysis has become the staple of undergraduate instruction in microeconomic principles.

Marshall's greatest book, *Principles of Economics*, was first published in 1890 and passed through eight editions before his death in 1924. He was born in 1842, only nineteen years after the death of David Ricardo. In 1884, he was appointed Professor of Political Economy at Cambridge but retired in 1908 to devote his life to writing. Marshall's conception of economics is portrayed by the Latin inscription on the title page of his *Principles*: *Natura non facit saltum*, meaning 'nature does not make a leap'. He regarded his work as analogous to that of Charles Darwin in that he sought to identify and to measure the laws of nature as these are revealed in economic activities.

The short period in the Marshallian system is the period during which the capitalist must hold a capital asset. He is required to do so because capital comes in 'lumps', like factories or machines. One might prefer, instead, to use only a portion of a building or of a machine, or to use it only for a short while. To do so today, one might negotiate a limited term lease. However, indicative of financing arrangements prevalent in Marshall's time, the typical asset was acquired only in exchange for a commitment to hold the asset to maturity in its entirety. The short period, or short run, is therefore a relative period of time, dictated by the character of the asset and by convention, during which ownership is 'fixed'. An asset so effected is called a fixed asset.

By contrast, variable inputs are those which can be added in varying quantities during the short period. For instance, in a simple two input-illustration, the variable input labour might be added in divisible quantities during the short period, whilst the fixed input – perhaps a factory – is constrained to enter as a 'lump' and to be present throughout the period. The short period continues until such time as the capitalist may determine that it may be expedient to terminate or sell the capital asset, perhaps selecting another in its place. Having acquired a replacement asset, the capitalist leaves one short period and enters into yet another short period.

Short periods are connected by Marshall's long period. The long period is a planning horizon over which the capitalist may select from among a variety of asset sizes, or short runs. Since asset size is constant in the short run, but can be varied in the long run according to the specifications of the capitalist, all inputs are considered to be variable in the long run.

In the short run the capitalist is obliged to use his asset in a way that maximizes his profit (or minimizes his loss). He is a captive of his circumstances which are initially self-imposed. Having acquired a capital asset and therefore being forced to retain it for the relevant period, he must make the most of his circumstances. The principal question facing him is: 'What is the profit maximizing rate of output associated with the capital asset, and therefore how many units of input labor must be hired per period to produce that output?' Clearly, the rational capitalist will not merely strive to minimize the cost associated with some quantity of production. Nor will he strive to maximize revenues associated with a certain quantity of goods produced and sold. Rather, he will select the profit-maximizing quantity of output such that the difference between total revenues and total costs is maximized.

The decision rule for setting the profit maximizing rate of profit in output markets is to set marginal cost equal to marginal revenue. In other words, the capitalist will continue to add output in each production period up to that point at which the extra revenue obtained by producing and selling one more unit is exactly offset by the extra cost of producing it.

THE DEMAND FOR LABOUR

Having determined the profit maximizing quantity of output, the capitalist proceeds to hire the profit maximizing quantity of variable input. The demand for input labour is said to be a 'derived demand'. Households demand finished goods and services, not labour. However, with the profit maximizing quantity of output known, which will be sold to households, then the demand for labour to be purchased from households can be calculated. In a competitive economy in which the typical firm faces a horizontal demand curve, the capitalist will maximize profit by continuing to add units of variable input

Table 6.1 Hourly production, cost and revenue data

1 Units of variable input	2 Total product	3 Marginal product	4 Product price	5 Total revenue	6 Marginal revenue product	7 Marginal factor cost
1	7	7	$2	$14	$14	$5
2	13	6	2	26	12	5
3	18	5	2	36	10	5
4	22	4	2	44	8	5
5	25	3	2	50	6	5
6	27	2	2	54	4	5
7	28	1	2	56	2	5

labour up to that point at which, for the last unit hired, the extra or marginal cost of the unit – called marginal factor cost (MFC) – is set equal to the value of the output created by that unit, which is called marginal revenue product (MRP). This is the universal decision rule for hiring variable inputs that is fully compatible with the profit maximizing condition – MC = MR – in output markets.

Note in Table 6.1 that marginal revenue product (MRP) in column 6 is obtained by calculating the total revenue (price times quantity) that is derived at each level of variable input use. Marginal revenue product therefore becomes the 'extra' revenue associated with the addition of an extra unit of input, added at the margin. Since we have assumed perfect competition to prevail, the capitalist can sell all units of output at a constant price. Also because of our competitive assumptions, he may purchase as many units of labour as he chooses at a constant wage. With regard to the decision rule, then, the capitalist will continue to add output, and therefore variable input labour, up to that point at which the extra or marginal cost associated with the last unit of input hired is just equal to its price.

Since each unit of variable input labour is homogeneous, each is considered to be equally motivated and skilled. The ability of the first worker hired to create a greater MRP than the second worker, and so on, is totally a function of the order of hire, and not of worker quality. Since each worker commands the same wage as any other in perfect competition, the decline in marginal product portrayed in column 3 relates entirely to the law of diminishing returns.[1]

The observation of particular significance is that the capitalist increases his profit when he hires back into the queue of potential workers, up to that point for the last worker hired, at which the extra revenue earned by increasing production just pays for the extra labour necessary to make it. We observe, then, that the last workers hired contribute very little to capitalist profit. But they do contribute something. Surely the addition to total profit associated with workers towards the front of the queue is much more attractive to the capitalist than it is for workers in the back. Even so, the capitalist is willing to retain and to pay the prevailing wage to the less profitable workers because in so doing he expands his total profit.

Let us assume that each worker in the illustration in Table 6.1 receives a wage of $5 an hour. This is shown in column 7 as marginal factor cost, or MFC. The first worker hired has a MRP of $14, so that worker adds $9 to profit ($14 MRP − $5 MFC). In the case of the fifth worker, his MFC of $5 is exceeded by a MRP of $6, for a net addition to capitalist profit of $1. Note that the first worker adds seven times as much to profit as does the fifth. Workers one to five, on average, contribute $5 each to profit. One might think that it would be rational to penalize workers four and five because they don't add as much as the 'average worker', number three, or the 'most productive workers', one and two. But this does not occur. The employer finds value in each one of the workers hired. Workers who are 'less productive' than the average are still attractive. Each one is valuable because each one contributes something to total profit, and therefore to growth. Even the worker who adds only a little profit still facilitates his employer's goal of profit maximization.

QUASI-RENT

The payment to assets held fixed during the Marshallian short period is called quasi-rent. It is the difference between total revenue and total variable cost. Alternately stated, it is the residual that accrues to the fixed input after the cost of the variable input (labour) has been paid. It is somewhat analogous to Ricardian or pure rent, which is the return to land or some other asset held permanently in fixed supply. Reorganization of the productive process can have no effect upon the quantity of a fixed asset drawing pure rent. In the Ricardian system, the use of fixed input land commands payment with or without the provision of industry, skill or risk. Land is a rentier asset.

Quasi-rent, on the other hand, is the payment to the fixed input in the Marshallian short period. Input fixity is only applicable to the short run. If the capitalist only breaks even in the short period, then quasi-rent is exactly equal to the cost of acquiring and holding the fixed input. If the capitalist earns a profit, then quasi-rent is equal to the cost of maintaining the fixed input, depreciation, and capitalist income. Note that the concept of quasi-rent implicitly assigns all increases in wealth to the fixed asset and to its manager, who is the capitalist. None of the increase in wealth is assigned to variable input labour in this system.

While the quantity of the asset may be fixed in the short run, its supply can be augmented in the long run. Hence, it receives payment because of its short-term scarcity value, but in the long run it does not command a scarcity premium. Scarcity is the key word here. Both asset scarcity and net profit disappear in the long run.

Conservation is the careful preservation and protection of something. Doctrinaire capitalism posits that society benefits from the conservation of privately held capital assets. Since capital is scarce, capitalists are motivated to acquire it and to conserve it to enrich society's material well-being. The reward to the capitalist is profit. The reward to society is the proliferation of a dynamic, rather than a static economy. Capital investment is ongoing, growth is positive, and wealth is consequently increasing.

The gross incentive to the capitalist entrepreneur, then, is the prospect of earning quasi-rent on an asset held in the short run. His net incentive is the prospect of net income, after payment of expenses. Expenses include the cost of the fixed input, capital consumption, and the cost of borrowed resources. It is the assertion of the doctrinaire system that an actual economy created in the likeness of the *laissez-faire* archetype will generate a positive amount of residual capitalist income in each period.

PROFIT MAXIMIZATION

Capital conservation, and therefore profit maximization, is a function of the rate of usage of the variable input. The rational capitalist will always expand output in the short run so long as the marginal revenue associated with selling one more unit exceeds the marginal cost of making it. In this manner quasi-rent on the fixed input, and total profit, are maximized. Even though the last unit of output may produce only a modicum of profit, it is wisdom for the capitalist to expand production to that point.

In so doing, however, the capitalist may actually lower the rate of profit, which is total profit divided by the quantity of output. Incremental expansion of output, accompanied by a very small expansion in total profit will drive the rate of profit lower. No matter. It is conceivable that total profit and the rate of profit could actually move in opposite directions. The doctrine asserts that it is not the rate of profit, or average profit, which the capitalist seeks to maximize, but rather total profit. Such behaviour is consonant with optimal asset conservation described by Alfred Marshall. Neither societal wealth nor capitalist income is maximized if the rate of profit on the fixed input, rather than total profit, is chosen for maximization instead.

Recall that the profit maximizing quantity of variable input, analogous to the profit maximizing quantity of output, can be obtained in the competitive model by setting marginal revenue product equal to marginal factor cost. In Table 6.1 the fifth worker hired adds only $1 to total profit. Consequently, he is retained to work in conjunction with the fixed capital asset because his efforts improve asset conservation, which is measured by the size of either total quasi-rent or total profit. Worker four, who adds $3 to total profit, is also retained.

Each of the last two workers in this example, while contributing to an increase in total profit, simultaneously contribute to a fall in the rate of profit. Let us consider the most productive workers. With only workers one and two employed, the average profit (MRPs of $14 plus $12, less MFC of $5 each) is $26 − 10, or $16, divided by two workers, which is $8. The addition of worker three lowers the rate of profit to $36 − 15, or $21, divided by three workers, which is $7 per worker. Of course, worker three in this example is the median profitable worker of seven workers. When worker number four is added, the rate of profit falls to $44 minus 20, or $24, divided by four workers, which is $6. And with worker five, average profitability of the workforce falls still further to $50 minus 25, or $25, divided by five workers, which is $5.

Our conclusion is that asset conservation in the short run is not enhanced by maximizing the rate of profit. Since quasi-rent and total profit are both measures of the efficient use of the fixed input, we conclude that setting rates of output and variable input usage so as to maximize the rate of profit is antithetic to the asset conservation ethic embodied in doctrinaire capitalism. Even so, we shall shortly acknowledge the second glitch of *laissez-faire* capitalism which blurs the distinction between these two variables. In so doing, application of

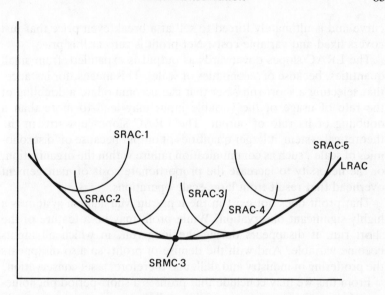

Figure 6.1 Short-run and long-run average cost curves with the short-run marginal cost curve for SRAC-3

the conventional wisdom may promote the underemployment of variable input labour.

LONG-RUN ANALYSIS

In the Marshallian long run (Figure 6.1) it is significant to recognize that there exists no profit at every point along the long-run average cost (LRAC). Several short-run average total cost curves (SRAC) are portrayed, and each is associated with a particular size of short-run capital asset. The LRAC is the 'envelope' of these short-run curves. Notice particularly the middle SRAC curve, SRAC-3. It is shown with its short-run marginal cost curve, which is the capitalist's short-run supply curve. A conclusion of Marshallian long-run analysis is that competition will drive the capitalist in the long run to select the size of capital asset that is associated with the minimum point on the LRAC. This is the size of asset for which per unit cost of operation is minimized. But because of competition we also acknowledge that the representative capitalist in the long run is forced down his supply curve and is ultimately forced to sell at a break even price that just covers fixed and variable costs. Net profit is zero at this price.

The LRAC slopes downwards as output is expanded, from small quantities, because of 'economies of scale'. This means, for instance, that selecting a short-run asset that can accommodate a doubling of the rate of usage of the variable input may lead to more than a doubling of its rate of output. The LRAC slopes upwards in the theoretical system at larger quantities of output because of 'diseconomies of scale', such as communication failure within the organization, or the necessity to increase the proportionate costs of management overhead that result from large-scale operations.

That profit does not exist in the long-run Marshallian system is a highly significant observation. While profit may be a feature of the short run, it disappears during the long run, in which all inputs become variable. And with the demise of profit, so also disappears the proffering of industry and skill, and therefore, asset conservation.

From this we may conclude that profit is a short-period phenomenon that results from actions of the capitalist to operative effectively and efficiently. Effective operation means that the capitalist produces the right product, so dictated by the market. Efficient operation means that the capitalist selects the appropriate size and mix of capital assets in the short-run and conserves these by producing at a rate that produces the maximum quantity of profit. Also, since the long run is associated with zero profit, its indefinite continuance would be indicative of the stationary state wherein net investment, profit, and therefore growth, have fallen to their zero levels.

A CURIOUSM

What we see before us is a glimpse of the manner in which the second glitch of doctrinal capitalism may be revealed. It is propelled by an anomaly in the application of conventional economic theory. That anomaly grows out of the disparity between optimal profit maximizing behaviour by capitalists, as prescribed by theory, and observations of actual profit maximizing behaviour by firms in the contemporary economic milieu.

We consider the possibility that firms may not observe the short-term convention of setting the rate of output commensurate with equality between marginal cost and marginal revenue. Rather, they may be motivated to maximize the rate of profit, and to thereby suboptimize output and employment in the Marshallian system. In input markets, this may be revealed by hiring substantially fewer units of variable input labour than portrayed by the equality of marginal revenue product with marginal factor cost. If the typical firm behaves in this manner, then each firm produces suboptimal quantities of output and employs a suboptimal quantity of variable input. In an extant economy, in which market power may be exercised by both buyers and sellers, the societal outcome of so behaving is a less-than-full-employment quantity of national output and employment.

Let us reconsider our illustration from Table 6.1. Here, the profit-maximizing quantity of variable input labour is five workers, even though the fifth worker adds only a small amount to total profit, and thereby lowers the rate of profitability associated with the fixed asset. Even so, the theory dictates that to hire fewer than five workers is irrational. However, to the extent that conditions prevailing in an extant economy may not reflect the assumptions of the theoretical archetype, then we may observe firms setting output and employment at theoretically irrational levels.

Such is the case in examples cited in Chapter 5. It is the rate of return on the placement of funds, and not total profitability associated with a given asset, that is often maximized in contemporary American capitalism. For instance, the first worker in Table 6.1 has the highest rate of profitability. For the five profitable workers combined, the aggregate rate of profit can be raised by discharging workers four and five. In so doing each remaining worker performs at or above the previous average profit rate.

Dismissing workers four and five appears as a particularly curious action in view of the conventional Marshallian prescription. Taken to 'the limit', this 'rate-raising' behaviour might even continue past the point of break even, incurring short-term losses. It would only end at that point at which quasi-rent is driven to zero, which is the shutdown point for the capitalist. For rates of operation below this point, not only is quasi-rent forfeited, but losses would be compounded because the cost of the variable input – the labour bill – would not be fully met.

How could this be? What might motivate a contemporary capitalist to operate in such a manner? We have observed that in the Marshallian long run, net profit is zero. In this situation the capitalist earns only a 'normal return' on his assets to maintain them in their present use. As such, the capitalist acts not as a capitalist but as a rentier. He provides neither skill nor industry, nor does he incur substantial risk. The capitalist class, in such a stationary society associated with continuous attainment of the long run, merely holds the stock of assets in existence, in a manner similar to the holding of land and other fixed assets by the rentier class in feudal society.

What we seek to investigate is the possibility of some theoretical glitch that may prescribe capitalist behaviour such that capitalists may not be compelled to enter the short run. Since net investment, profit and growth are conditional upon the attainment of the short run, the failure to embrace it, and therefore the perpetual attainment of the long run, would result in the attainment of stationary society.

Is there such a glitch embedded in economic theory? We propose that there is. Its effect is to hold the modern firm, operating in the contemporary milieu, on its planning horizon such that it may never ascend the short run. Consequently, it may never act as a capitalist. In so doing, we observe a second tragedy of the commons, which is the fallacy of wealth creation. An individual transactor may optimize her wealth position by maximizing the rate of return on the placement of her funds, rather than maximizing the total profitability associated with each asset. In so doing the welfare of an isolated transactor may be enhanced. But when this behaviour becomes accepted as 'best practice', the societal outcome is the failure to attain the short run. Consequently, capitalists as a class will not invest and wealth will not be created. This outcome is particularly deleterous to doctrinaire *laissez-faire*, because the intellectual justification of *laissez-faire* is based upon the ability of extant economies modelled in the capitalist archetype to obtain continuing, politically satisficing rates of net investment and real growth.

7 Profit Lacuna

Recall in Ricardo's system the significance of equality between saving and investment. It is a condition of equilibrium embedded in the comparative static method. In equilibrium, all opposing forces in a system are cancelled out. Without a change in some system parameter, we would expect the status quo to prevail in perpetuity. In economics, there are only two cases in which saving and investment equality may remain constant over time. Both are steady states.

Steady state one is the special case of the stationary state in which growth, profit and net investment are zero. Saving is equal to gross investment. But these are equal to depreciation, or capital consumption. Current period saving is completely exhausted by depreciation. In other words, in the stationary state society saves only and exactly the amount necessary to replace capital consumed in current production. The outcome is a perpetuation of the status quo with regard to asset and output composition.

Steady state one is ideologically incompatible with the *laissez-faire* doctrine. Net investment and growth must exist for private enterprise to be justified. In stationary society, the only justification for the private ownership of assets – and for any particular distribution of those assets amongst the population – is the precedent of the status quo. Since net investment is zero, a class of capitalists does not exist. Those who control the placement of assets in stationary society are rentiers.

The economic system is dynamic in steady state two. Net investment, profit and growth are present. So also is a class of capitalists. The rate of growth of net investment specifies the long-term growth path of the economic system. Of course, the rate of real growth in the model can be anything we would like it to be. The problem is in determining what it shall be. In the conventional system it is not specified endogenously by the theory. Rather, it must be set exogenously, by some convention, or by explicit societal determination. It is indeterminate in the theoretical system.

MARGINALIST REVOLUTION

We have considered the environment in which Adam Smith and David Ricardo wrote. Smith preceded the Industrial Revolution, whereas Ricardo wrote during its early manifestations. Both were born into an agrarian culture that was beginning its transition into an industrial culture. Although professional opinion varies somewhat with regard to the exact dates of the Industrial Revolution, we may reasonably assume that the revolution was under way by the turn of the nineteenth century, and that it was essentially complete by the time of the American Civil War, in the mid-1860s.

Before the Industrial Revolution, the central issue of political economy was enhancing the 'wealth of nations' by improving national living standards. But by the 1870s, which marks the beginning decade of the neoclassical revolution in economics, the goal was shifting away from wealth creation, towards seeking an understanding of the workings of the price rationing mechanism. It was value, or price, rather than wealth creation, that was becoming the focus of economic inquiry.

Certainly the traditional capitalist societies of the late nineteenth century had not achieved the fabled 'golden age' in which all human beings become materially satiated. But the industrial revolution had resulted in substantial, aggregate improvement in living standards. Doctrinaire capitalism had been politically validated by extant economic growth. And, having demonstrated substantial progress towards that end, popular intellectual inquiry turned from that which appeared to be working successfully, to that which remained unknown.

Neoclassical scholars were concerned to develop a theory of value. Unlike their classical forebears, however, the neoclassicists appealed not to logic and the deductive method, but to the powerful force of nascent social science. Their observations were empirical, and their approach was that of positivist inquiry. All knowledge must be verifiable in sensory human experience. The *a priori* method of David Ricardo had fallen from vogue. Since it was deductive, its conclusions were therefore presumptive: they were derived by reasoning from certain self-evident principles. In the twentieth century the insights upon which such principles are based are often labelled as empirically unverifiable generalizations. Direct observation has precluded logical inference as the respected intellectual method of contemporary social inquiry.

NATURAL LAW

Even though their method of inquiry was dramatically altered from the method of the classicists, the neoclassical scholars shared a common methodological interest with their intellectual forebears. It was a passion for order as it may be revealed in natural law. Alfred Marshall cast his inquiry into human behaviour in the same mode as Charles Darwin's inquiry into the origin of species. His quest was to discover the laws of nature as these may be revealed in human economic behaviour.

Nowhere is this quest to discover the order of natural law more apparent than in the preface to *The Distribution of Wealth*, published by John Bates Clark in 1899. Clark was an American economist who is credited with developing some of the most powerful synthesizing statements of the neoclassical period. Clark was unabashed about his purpose in the preface to his masterwork. It was none other than 'to show that the distribution of the income of society is controlled by a natural law, and that this law, if it worked without friction, would give to every agent of production the amount of wealth which that agent creates'.

We shall shortly consider the profound implications of the dependence of twentieth-century empirical method in economics upon an eighteenth-century natural law view.

STATIONARY SOCIETY

The quest for theoretical elegance in the discovery of the laws of nature as they operate upon commerce led the neoclassical scholars to a curious position. As they solidified their intellectual apparatus, they selected a vision of world order in which net investment is zero. Growth has ceased in the system and the class of capitalists does not exist. Population is presumed to be constant. Everyone in the neoclassical vision of the ideal society is comfortable with consuming this year's quantity of real output into perpetuity. Consequently, the stock of assets that society holds in this hypothetical system is the stock that it chooses to hold indefinitely. There are no forces operating to create economic change. It is the stationary version of the steady state which the neoclassical scholars chose as the basis of their intellectual system.

But why did they choose the stationary state, in preference to a model with a steady state rate of net investment and growth? They did so because of the elegance that can be developed from its assumptions, and because its use did not require any exogenous specification of the rate of growth and profit. These are implicit within the model. In the neoclassical system it is not necessary to specify what the rate of profit is, for it is zero.

In the context in which Marshall, Clark and their contemporaries worked and wrote, the exclusion of growth, profit and everything related to it was not an important omission. After all, in their time economic growth had come to be treated as a given in extant capitalist economies. Since growth was no longer a driving force of public policy, it was safe in their time to develop a pure theory of choice that made no reference to a pre-industrial growth problem. Their quest was to create a paradigm capable of explaining value.

There exists a problem, however, in using that paradigm in the contemporary era. For in the latter part of the twentieth century growth is re-emerging as a substantial public policy concern. No longer are extant capitalist economies considered to grow as a normal and continuing consequence of their establishment on *laissez-faire* principles. What is needed today is an economic paradigm that allows economists and the public once again to ask and answer questions which pertain to wealth creation. But what is available for our use is the conventional wisdom of neoclassical theory in which economic growth is ignored, *ceteris paribus*. Unfortunately, attempts to deal with questions of economic growth are likely to be rendered sterile by a paradigm which disavows not only their significance but their very existence.

CAPITAL À LA WALRAS

The neoclassical system was cast in a stationary *Weltanschauung* by the Cambridge scholar A.C. Pigou. Further refinements were taken by John Bates Clark of Columbia University. It was Clark who is credited with the full pedagogical development of the neoclassical synthesis, and therefore its promulgation as the prevailing theory of price and value.

Professor Pigou accepted the challenge of rationalizing two disparate views of the supply of capital. The first way is associated with Léon Walras and David Ricardo in which the relative prices of commodities are determined by the market forces of supply and demand. According to Joan Robinson (1971, p. 13), the quantity of capital in this scheme is 'a list of stocks of fully specified means of production'. It is depicted as 'a great collection of various kinds of equipment, stocks and works in progress'. Capital assets are not measured in dollars. Rather, each is described with regard to its kind and quality, the nature of variable inputs that it uses, etc.

The British economist Wicksteed (1894, p. 33) was clear on this point. 'Instead of speaking of so many pounds [sterling] of capital,' he said, 'we shall speak of so many ploughs . . . and so many horses.' This definition of the supply of capital is compatible with the Smithian and Ricardian distinction between productive and non-productive asset use. But the problem with this scheme is that it provides no way of accounting for the rate of profit on capital. Since the supply of capital has no common denominator (money is missing), it cannot be aggregated. Therefore, the rate of profit on capital – which is profit divided by asset cost for a given period – can only be specified in physical units. Rate of return comparisons across various classes of assets are therefore made extremely cumbersome.

CAPITAL À LA MARSHALL

The second scheme for treating the supply of capital was introduced by Alfred Marshall and was later formalized by Professor Pigou. In this formulation, assets are not merely enumerated, instead they are denominated in dollars (or other currency). A capitalist may thus specify so many dollars of asset value in ploughs, in horses, etc. Each quantity of an asset has a supply price which is the price that must be paid to call forth that amount. This price measures the efforts and sacrifices of capitalists and workers.

The Marshallian scheme has two distinct advantages over the first. Since each asset has a supply price in terms of a unit of money (pound sterling or dollars), it becomes possible to aggregate unlike units. So, while it is impossible meaningfully to add a given number of horses with a given number of ploughs, it is quite feasible to add the dollar value of each to obtain an aggregate value for the stock of capital. The second advantage is that the payment for capital can be computed as a value per unit of value, rather than as a value per unit of a physical service, such as a horse or a plough. This facilitates comparisons among various classes of capital assets in order to select prospectively those with the highest rates of return. It also facilitates profitability comparisons such as between acquiring a new asset or refurbishing and expanding an existing one.

THE DILEMMA

The Marshallian schema is better suited for a complex economy with money, in comparison with the Walrasian system which lends itself to barter. But the problem with the Marshallian scheme, in spite of its apparent convenience, is that within it the distinction between productive and non-productive asset use becomes meaningless. In the Walrasian scheme, in which each kind and quality of asset is individually enumerated, it is possible to distinguish between assets that are invested and those that are held merely to benefit rentier consumption. We cannot know if an asset is being used productively unless we can investigate the use to which it is put.

Let us consider this crucial point further. The Marshallian schema provides a link to factor markets in which asset values may be determined competitively. Asset values in the Walrasian schema, on the other hand, are intrinsic to the asset. We must observe the conditions of its use. So if the asset is sold in a competitive market and subsequently converted to a different use, we cannot know the portion of the asset selling price that compensates the capitalist. We therefore lose sight of the distinction between capitalist income and rentier income.

Also, suppose the capitalist attempts to optimize his position by choosing prospectively between investing in one more unit of corn, or investing in the breeding of draft horses instead. Let's assume that the husbanding outcome at the end of the current period is likely to be the birth of a foal. Herein lies the problem. How is the capitalist able prospectively to ascertain the benefit to his wealth position that comes from committing a new act of investment in grain (farming), or alternatively committing a new act of investment in husbandry? There exists no standard in the Walrasian system by which these two activities can be objectively compared. Since the prospective grain payment can only be compared to the prospective payment of 'horse flesh' in physical units, how is the optimizing capitalist to know which choice will better advance his wealth position?

An even more complex problem involves intratemporal comparisons. Suppose, for instance, that the grain investment earns its reward in a single year, whereas it may take two years for the husbandry investment to reach fruition. Since we are limited in the Walrasian schema to calculating asset payments in physical units, how are we able to choose intelligently between different classes of assets which are also associated with different intratemporal payment flows?

This problem resolves nicely in the Marshallian schema. Since the value of all assets, and all asset payments, are computed in a common standard of value – money – either the capitalist or the rentier can objectively compare the attractiveness of alternative placements. And since the Marshallian schema permits measurement in 'value per unit of value', it lends itself to the calculation of compound interest, and it therefore facilitates intratemporal comparisons of asset ownership.

But notice the problem implicit in the use of the more sophisticated Marshallian schema, with money and with complex markets. For example, if the team of horses is sold in a complex and formal market, how are we to know the portion of the sale price that compensates the efforts of the capitalist, *qua* capitalist, versus that portion which merely compensates the capitalist *qua* rentier? In the Walrasian formulation we could compare the return to comparable teams of horses that are loaned out, or that are held as investment assets. The comparison would enable us to assign a value to profit, or capitalist income. We could also perform the same observation in the Marshallian schema, so long as we did not lose track of individual assets and their uses.

Of course, the power of the Marshallian schema is in its ability to denominate unlike assets in a common measure of value, and therefore to aggregate them. So, even though we might record the use value of an asset, although its value might be denominated in dollars, such observations are likely to be lost in accounting for the inner workings of a complex market economy with money. As aggregation occurs, and the supply of capital is lumped together, the use value of individual assets becomes obscure. So also do the efforts of capitalists and rentiers – and therefore their rewards – become obscure.

THE SYNTHESIS

Each of the two schemes presented for resolution in the neoclassical synthesis was accompanied by specific utilities and disutilities of use. Joan Robinson (1964) points out that it was A.C. Pigou who reconciled the Walrasian and the Marshallian views of the supply of capital. The synthesis was fundamental to the development of a coherent theory of distribution. Of particular interest to neoclassical scholars was to distinguish the rightful share going to the classes of capitalists, rentiers and labourers.

Factor shares, which specify how earned income should be distributed among resource providers, obviously differ in the Walrasian and Marshallian formulations. The latter requires no payment to capitalists. In the Marshallian system, the only reward to the asset-holder is the reward for 'waiting to consume'. Marshall's view was that asset-holders are only willing to commit their wealth, and therefore to forego current consumption, in anticipation of an economic reward. Their payment is the value of waiting, and it is just sufficient to motivate them to forego immediate gratification. There are no other rewards or incentives to hold capital assets in the Marshallian system.

The similarity between Marshall's reward for waiting and Ricardo's rentier consumption is inescapable. In fact, they are identical. If the Marshallian capitalist is not compensated beyond the level of the Ricardian rentier, then they become one and the same. The Marshallian reward for waiting only compensates rentier consumption, and provides no additional incentive to encourage capitalist skill and industry and risk-taking.

What we conclude about the Marshallian system for treating the supply of capital is that it contains no profit reward to the capitalist, and therefore no capitalist. Neither does it contain net investment or growth. It is a portrayal of a static society in which households are assumed to be content to hold exactly the stock of assets in existence.

Marshall's paradigm is built upon a very different world view from the paradigm of Adam Smith and David Ricardo, portrayed by Léon Walras. We have observed that no longer is the quest to explain and to predict economic growth. Rather, the focus of the neoclassical revolution is to explain and to predict value. Growth in the Marshallian system is treated *ceteris paribus*: that is, it is assumed to be held constant and therefore out of the range and consequence of the analytical model.

The Marshallian system was definitely more attractive to the popular interests of Western capitalist economies in the early decades of the twentieth century. It was better suited to the complexity of sophisticated capital markets and the use of complex money. Its focus was upon an explanation of value. Its fault with regard to issues of growth was consistent with the perspective of the times, which treated growth as an innate characteristic of capitalism. Even if the profession adopted a model devoid of a theory of growth, it was implicitly assumed that the growth-oriented character of the Industrial Revolution would continue to produce unbounded prosperity for nations that subscribed to the doctrine.

DISTRIBUTION

The advantage of the marginal productivity theory of distribution was its elegance and power. Since it does not differentiate between capitalist and rentier, it supports a powerful theorem which says that in an optimal situation, any dollar of an asset or other productive resource should receive a constant rate of return in its marginal use. Implicit in the dicta is a powerful judgement of value that a capital asset should receive no greater reward than a rentier asset. No distinction is made with regard to asset use.

Since the Marshallian paradigm fits the cultural issues of the time more closely than its competitor, it was featured in the synthesis. The two opposing views were ultimately reconciled by specifying a zero rate of profit in the Walrasian system. Thus it was assumed that net investment and growth could be held at zero without consequence upon the development of the neoclassical theory of value. According to this convention, the Walrasian system contains a capitalist who does not function as such. His only reward is the reward for waiting, which is the reward of the rentier.

Perhaps we can now make some sense of our original question in this chapter about the choice of steady state two – the stationary state – over steady state one, or equilibrium with a constant rate of growth. Surely the choice is rooted in the goal of Cartesian science, which is power and control over the environment. The Marshallian view provided great explanatory power in the late nineteenth and early twentieth centuries, not only because of its scientific theory of value, but also because it allowed the nascent science of economics to make elaborate claims of being 'ideologically neutral', or 'value free'.

However, implicit within the precision of the neoclassical system is a natural law theory of distribution. Factor shares are distributed according to a presumption which is entirely metaphysical in its character. The return from one dollar's worth of any asset should equal the return to one dollar's worth of any other. If it is a capital asset, still it receives no higher rate of return than a rentier asset. Unfortunately, the failure consciously to recognize the metaphysical basis upon which the value dicta of the neoclassical theory rests, severely limits its practical usefulness. This is particularly true with regard to questions of wealth creation, such as those plaguing mature capitalist economies in the late twentieth century, and those problems that have plagued developing economies since the inception of trade.

The framework of the marginal productivity theory of distribution, which is an extension of the neoclassical system, is the demand for and the supply of factors to individual firms. Each firm in a perfectly competitive environment is governed by the profit maximizing dicta that it will hire units of a variable factor in the short run up to that point at which the marginal revenue product (MRP) of the factor is equal to factor cost. Thus the typical firm acting under conditions of perfect competition continues to hire units of the variable factor so long as the revenue associated with the employment of the last unit exceeds the cost of that unit. And the marginal revenue product curve of the firm becomes its demand curve for the variable factor. Marginal revenue product theory is frequently described as employment theory, since it specifies the price and quantity combinations at which the rational firm will hire variable input labour.

Together, the payment to the variable factor labour and the residual payment to the fixed factor land are identically equal to the value of total product created by the combined use of the two factors. Or, the combination of the two factors could be reversed with the same result. Using labour as the fixed factor in the short run and adding increments of variable factor land, the value of the payment to land is obtained. The residual, then, constitutes the payment to labour. In the neoclassical system, payments to the two factors will be identical in either method of calculation.

EULER'S THEOREM

A powerful theorem of neoclassical distribution theory is known as the 'Adding Up', or Euler's Theorem. It states that the total product is exactly exhausted by factor rewards equal to their marginal products. Rima (1978) indicates that it was Swedish economist Knut Wicksell who pointed out that the Adding Up Theorem only works if the production function is homogeneous and linear, or if the presence of pure competition causes the firm to achieve optimum size in the long run.

But in an actual economy in which economies of scale, externalities, and market power may be present, the marginal productivity theory of distribution is not likely to describe actual patterns of distribution. It could work in a steady state system, however, without friction or time, if all production functions are homogeneous and linear. Otherwise, its usefulness as a prescriptive tool of public policy analysis is extremely limited. That is, it has normative value only to the extent that an actual economy conforms completely with the highly structured assumptions upon which the vision of the neoclassical world is based. In an actual economy, the sum of the marginal products of the various factors is likely to exceed or to be exceeded by the value of total product, thereby violating the theorem. What we see in neoclassical distribution theory, then, is a special case, built upon highly qualified assumptions which are not likely to be fulfilled in an actual economy.

Even so, the neoclassical economists used this highly specialized intellectual system as the basis for what, in reality, is an ethical system prescribing the distribution of wealth. The attempt is not only to formulate natural laws of income distribution, but to place distribution squarely within the realm of ethics. According to Professor Clark, the system produces a theory of value that would be representative 'if the consolidating of capital were to cease and if the wants of consumers were never to alter'. These 'prices', according to Clark, 'are the theoretically "natural" rates which science has been seeking'.

Here we clearly see the intellectual heritage of the neoclassical system as it has embedded within it a distribution system based upon natural law. That we may accept the value judgements implicit within that vision is a metaphysical ascendancy, and as such it is legitimate to scholarly inquiry. But to the extent that an empirical science may be built up from its foundations, and ethical prescriptions for distribution made under the guise and protection of science, then the ascendancy of faith implied therein becomes truly heroic.

If the rich axioms of the neoclassical system become lost to our constant, penetrating view, then we also lose sight of the careful limits that must be placed upon the questions which we may ask and answer within the framework of the received theory. To assert, then, that orthodox economic science is value free, is to operate in total disregard of the intellectual apparatus of the economist's heritage.

HEROIC ASSUMPTIONS

The marginal productivity theory of distribution justifies that if a factor is compensated according to the value of the marginal product which it creates, then it is receiving a just payment. Thus, in equilibrium, Clark's system prescribes that a dollar's worth of any input should receive the same rate of return as a dollar's worth of any other input. Alternately stated, the specific conclusion of this system is that a dollar's worth of capital commands the same rate of return as a dollar's worth of a rentier asset. But this flagrantly disregards the extra skill, risk and industry of holding capital. To support this dicta of orthodox distribution theory, then, is to obviate a role and a reward for capital as separate from rentier assets. To so act is to totally disregard the animus of capitalism, which is economic growth.

Unfortunately, Clark's heroic assumptions become buried under an elegant superstructure which has been erected by microeconomists upon his analytic summary. That structure is highly useful to the theoretical determination of value, and therefore to the study of individual choice under specific conditions. But it is at the same time extremely limited in the types of problems to which it can be applied. To the extent that this ethically biased system is used as a prescriptive device for wealth creation, then economists become gullible victims as well as perpetrators of a theory of distribution based upon the assumptions of natural law.

RENT AND FINANCE

Through the use of an extrapolation of Ricardo's system, we have been able to make an articulate distinction between profit and rent on the basis of productive and non-productive asset use. Now we must further distinguish between classes of rentier assets. In the Walrasian system, a rentier asset earns value measured in physical units of that asset. Like Ricardo's, the system of Walras contains no money. When we replace barter with the complexity of money in the Marshallian system, however, we must account for a new class of rentier assets.

This new class of rentier assets is called finance. Like the placement of an asset for rentier consumption, finance is similarly non-productive. Its holder may do so without proffering skill or industry, and without incurring substantial risk. Unlike rentier assets, the reward to financial placements is not accounted in physical units of the asset. Rather, the reward to finance is interest, which is measured in the Marshallian system as a value per unit of a value.

The profit lacuna implicit in the neoclassical synthesis decrees that each dollar of an asset, regardless of its use, shall receive the same rate of return. We have observed in the classical systems of Ricardo and Walras that the lack of a reward to a class of capitalists causes a blurring of the distinction between capitalist and rentier assets. Profit, net investment and growth are absent in the vision of the neoclassical synthesis. Consequently, capitalists become reduced to a class of rentiers which merely maintains some constant stock of assets from period to period.

Now we broaden the implications of the profit lacuna, and extend it from the general class of rentier assets to the specific class of finance. In the Marshallian system, both capital and finance receive payment as value per unit of value. But in the absence of a theory of what the rate of profit should be, and therefore by setting it at its default value of zero, capital and financial assets become homogenized. The rate of return on assets held by the defunct class of capitalists is no greater than the rate of return on assets held by financiers. The rate of finance may become erroneously called the rate of profit in a stationary economy with complex money and sophisticated markets. But it is none other than the prevailing rate of interest, which is the money value of some fixed quantity of rentier assets.

Recall that we have defined the payment to capital as the reward to skill, industry and risk-taking, above the payment to holding the asset stock in some non-productive use. The payment to the latter is rent or interest, which is the reward for waiting in the Marshallian system. Arbitrage between the markets for rentier assets and the more specialized markets for finance equalize the rates of return from these two asset classes.

Only one of the three components of the service rendered by the capitalist can be innately valued in the Marshallian system. Since it is possible for the financier to receive the reward for waiting to consume without proffering skill or industry, we would expect these virtues to be lost as we shift from the classical world to the neoclassical world view. Only risk is likely to be compensated in the Marshallian system because it can be measured and allocated. Risk is the chance of loss, and it can be measured. An insurance company, for instance, may calculate the probability of an insured losing his life or property in a given year. Rates can be assigned accordingly. Each insured bears some fixed portion of the risk associated with the class of insureds to which they belong.

So also can arbitrage between asset classes assign a risk premium to the holding of certain assets. For instance, two classes of financial assets may be valued in their respective markets, and differentiated in price according to the risk involved in holding each. But the existence of a risk premium on a particular class of assets does not necessarily decree that the risk premium should be equated with profit. Risk is only one component of profit. It is the only profit component that can be assigned a value in the Marshallian system. However, because the risk component of capitalist service can be so valued, one should use great discretion in the Marshallian model not to equate the risk premium with the compensation of the full range of capitalist services.

OPTIMIZING

The blurring of the distinction between capital and finance in the neoclassical system, and therefore the blurring of profit and interest, may lead to a condition in an extant economy wherein profit, net investment and growth essentially disappear. Since the entrepreneur can be compensated at the same rate by operating as a rentier or financier, as by operating as a capitalist, he will rationally opt for the less costly path. Since only one of the three elements of capitalist service – risk – can be valued, the market value of common assets is likely to differ only by the size of the risk premium attached to their present use. Skill and industry are not compensated, and therefore asset-holders are motivated to hold their wealth conservatively. Since only a portion of profit and therefore net investment is equal to the value of the risk premium, the Marshallian system is asserted to be compatible with a shortage of investment capital in an extant economy.

How could this be? Our immediate quest is to consider how an individual transactor, following the optimizing dicta of the Marshallian system, could invoke the tragedy of the commons. Specifically, in attempting to make his own wealth position larger, is it possible that if everyone acted as prescribed, that societal wealth could be held stationary, or even decrease?

This could occur in an extant economy if transactors follow the prevailing dicta, which is spelled out in the specializations of managerial economics and finance. Contemporary schools of professional management instruct that it is the overall rate of profit on all asset holdings, and not the total quantity of profit associated with each individual asset, that should be maximized. Optimizing dictates that finance should be allocated prospectively, among scarce and competing uses according to the opportunity cost principle. The opportunity cost of obtaining rate of return B on asset 2, is the money value of the higher rate of return, A, that could have been earned on competing asset 1. Retrospectively, the transactor could have improved his outcome by taking a larger position in asset 1, and by forgoing 'investment' in asset 2.

The above strategy is rational for a single transactor. But the problem comes if all transactors pursue similar optimizing strategies, given an economic model that contains no innate reward for holding capital, and in an extant environment with complex money and sophisticated markets. Transactors will pay for skill and industry only if they are economically motivated to do so. In the Marshallian system they may not be so motivated.

Recall that in the Marshallian system, that net investment, profit and growth occur only in the short period. The Marshallian long run is indicative of stationary society. In the prevailing society of Alfred Marshall, asset-holders were required by convention to acquire and to hold capital in lumps, and to fruition. However, to the extent that a contemporary economy may permit transactors to 'keep their options open' by continuously shifting wealth among assets, then it may also be possible for them to avoid conserving capital in the short run.

The outcome, as we shall consider further in the next chapter, may be the attainment of the very vision of the neoclassical world view, which is the stationary state. As such, it constitutes a glitch in economic theory. That theory may have served adequately in another era. But with changes in the market economies of the late twentieth century – particularly as transactors may be able to avoid the short run by avoiding any time commitment to the asset – the implicit assumption of continuous economic growth may not be realized. And the anomalous consequence may be that in pursuit of the dicta of the *laissez-faire* system, that rather than obtaining an increase in the wealth of nations, that the 'zero sum' outcome of traditional society emerges instead.

MARGINAL EFFICIENCY OF CAPITAL

Professor Robinson points out that it was also Keynes who cleared up the confusions of the neoclassical economists between the rate of profit and the rate of interest. The problem actually becomes a distinction between the return on real investment accruing to entrepreneurs and the cost of borrowing which influences the return on loaned finance. Keynes's argument was cast in the form of a model of profit expectations which he called the marginal efficiency of capital (MEC). It is an estimate of future returns to be obtained on investments in productive capacity.

The marginal efficiency of capital indicates the rate of return expected from each potential capital placement. By calculating the difference between the MEC, and the cost of finance which is the rate of interest (*r*) the firm must pay on borrowed finance, we obtain the rate of return or the rate of profit. Thus, if the MEC is 20 per cent and *r* is 15 per cent, a rate of return of 5 per cent is expected. The MEC, then, enables a specification of the difference between the cost of finance, which is the rate of return on non-productive rentier-held assets, and the higher rate of return on productively held capitalist assets which reward for entrepreneurial industry, skill and the acceptance of risk.

Investment decisions for all possible projects are made in this manner. The firm estimates the MEC associated with each project under consideration, as demonstrated in the schedule in Figure 7.1. Here we assume that the firm holds an existing stock of capital net of depreciation of $300 000. Project I, then, requires the commitment of $100 000 of new investment and is viable for any rate of interest below 20 per cent. Project III, in comparison, requires $200 000 of new investment and it is viable for any rate of interest below 10 per cent. Given a hypothetical rate of interest of 16 per cent, the firm initiates only Project I for a net rate of return of 4 per cent. If the rate of interest falls to 12 per cent, then the firm initiates Projects I and II, respectively.

But in spite of Keynes's clarification of the distinction between profit and interest, the neo-neoclassics who followed Keynes, as Robinson (1971, pp. 32–3) identifies them, 'slipped back into the habit of identifying the rate of profit with the rate of interest and reasserted the doctrine that the rate of return measures the marginal productivity of capital from the point of view society as a whole, without attempting to explain what it means'.

According to Professor Robinson, it was J.B. Clark who provided the clearest articulation of the neoclassical 'scheme of ideas . . . intended to present an industrial economy as a scene of rationality and social harmony under the guidance of the "hidden hand" of competitive market forces . . . What a social class gets, is, under natural law, what it contributes to the general output of industry.'

'The neo-neoclassical revival of pre-Keynesian theory,' according

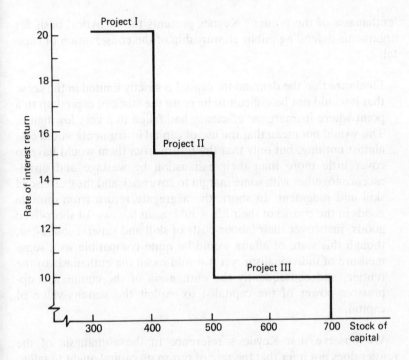

Figure 7.1 The marginal efficiency of capital schedule for a firm (in thousands of dollars)

to Professor Robinson, 'took over J.B. Clark's identification of capital as profit-earning finance with capital as a stock of means of production . . . The "rewards" to the factors correspond to their "marginal productivities".' The outcome of this lack of clarity 'seems to be a confusion between the idea of productivity of investment and the productivity of "capital"'.

HIGH INTEREST RATES

Keynes (1936, pp. 375–6) explicitly expressed his dissatisfaction with the moral implications surrounding the blurring of the distinction between the return to capital and the return to loaned finance. 'Interest today rewards no genuine sacrifice,' he argued, 'any more than does the rent of land.' In his now famous passage advocating the 'euthanasia of the rentier', Keynes presents the analytical basis for arguments defending public stewardship of the conservation of capital:

> I feel sure that the demand for capital is strictly limited in the sense that it would not be difficult to increase the stock of capital up to a point where its marginal efficiency had fallen to a very low figure. This would not mean that the use of capital instruments would cost almost nothing, but only that the return from them would have to cover little more than their exhaustion by wastage and obsolescence together with some margin to cover risk and the exercise of skill and judgment. In short, the aggregate return from durable goods in the course of their life would, as in the case of short-lived goods, just cover their labour-costs of skill and supervision. Now, though this state of affairs would be quite compatible with some measure of individualism, yet it would mean the euthanasia of the rentier, and consequently the euthanasia of the cumulative oppressive power of the capitalist to exploit the scarcity-value of capital.

We observe that Keynes's reference to the euthanasia of the rentier does not infer that the rate of return on capital ought to fall to zero, as some interpretations of this passage have suggested. A zero rate of return on finance is perfectly compatible with a positive rate of return on capital. Of course, a positive rate of return on finance is also compatible with a zero rate of return on capital.

What concerns us here is the prospect that an extant economy might attain the stationary state as the marginal efficiency of society's aggregate stock of capital falls to zero, because of high real interest rates. If the cost of finance rises to a level at which net investment is zero and only capital consumed in current production is replaced, then the reward to investment is zero. Those who hold society's stock of assets under such conditions function merely as rentiers or financiers.

8 Zero Sum Society

> The American government offers no direction. Steelmakers don't invest. Banks won't lend. And elite managers who graduate from business schools only engage in money games.[1]

The operating environment of the typical firm in the late twentieth century is very different from the prevailing environment described by Alfred Marshall nearly a century ago. Marshall wrote near the end of the industrial revolution, which transformed agricultural society during the nineteenth century into a society of manufacturers. The individual entrepreneur had not yet given way to the modern stock company. Research and product development mainly proceeded at the initiative of individuals, rather than large organizations. Management science as a discipline did not exist, and the hand of government was not ever-present in its attempts to redistribute or to improve market efficiency.

Nineteenth-century entrepreneurs were unable to avoid holding tangible capital for extended periods, and therefore they were compelled to act consistent with the Marshallian short period. Convention required the capitalist to act deliberately to obtain and to hold an asset, over its life, and in its entirety. Certainly the risk of ownership could not be mitigated by dividing a discrete capital asset into small portions to be held simultaneously by many individuals. Convention also required that the capitalist act as his own manager, rather than delegating that management role to a subordinate.

But in the United States a major reorganization of capitalist society was occurring around the turn of the twentieth century. The outcome was a change in the prevailing business environment which made it very different from the environment which prevailed in Marshall's youth. Perhaps the most significant decade of this transformation in America occurred in the 1880s. A.A. Berle and G. C. Means (1932) reported that it was quite complete at the time of their research. This transformation was the shift from individual capitalists as the prevailing owners, to ownership by large stock corporations which employ professional managers to perform operational responsibilities. In the contemporary business environment, managers often hold significant blocks of stock themselves, or acquire ownership rights through profit-sharing programmes.

105

To illustrate, almost one quarter of national income earned in America between 1900 and 1909 was earned by proprietorships – the independently owned and operated enterprises described in Marshall's paradigm. But the 1970s, in comparison, the share earned by proprietorships had slipped to a mere 7 per cent.

CONTEMPORARY MANAGEMENT

Today, the typical American works in a complex organization rather than a proprietorship. Certainly the contemporary image of 'organization man' stands in stark contrast to the vision of the proprietary firm portrayed by neoclassical theory. If the organization is a private sector organization, it is likely to be a publicly held corporation owned by a myriad of shareholders and managed by professionals trained in management science. Equity and finance are raised in complex markets and in immense quantities. Specialists provide expertise in complex fields such as marketing, banking, law, organization analysis, etc.

Often large institutions, and not individuals, are the dominant owners. They spread their assets across many organizations to minimize the risk of any single venture. And they may trade in mammoth blocks of equity or finance, perhaps sheltering their positions by quickly shifting their holdings among assets or asset classes. The professional managers who administer these complex organizations are not likely to be skilled in the production activities of the businesses which they oversee. It is the broadly applicable skills of financial management, and not the specific skills of production, that characterize the current generation of American managers.

Theirs is a perilous environment. The performance period for their organizations – the period over which stockholders and analysts judge their effectiveness – is typically the calendar quarter. Product lines must be developed, produced and marketed within the context of continuing quarter-to-quarter scrutiny. Weak quarterly financial performance, possibly resulting from a strategy to trade longer term for more popular short-term objectives, may prove destabilizing to the firm. If quarterly earnings fall, stock prices may also fall to undervalue the firm's assets, possibly precipitating a raid in which the firm's assets are reorganized or even liquidated. For these and other reasons the contemporary manager is induced to concentrate energies in the present, and possibly to underemphasize longer term strategies.

Henry F. Myers recently commented on the front page of the 10 February 1986 *Wall Street Journal* about the proclivity of American management towards short-term thinking:

> a lot of the widely hailed restructuring of American industry is actually mere asset shuffling. Factories change hands but don't change for the better . . . many American managers still show an unhealthy preoccupation with short-term objectives, with financial coups rather than with what is happening on the factory floor.
>
> They are pushed toward short-term thinking partly by securities analysts and professional money managers, who constantly press for ever-higher profits, quarter by quarter. And in the current wave of corporate takeovers and leveraged buyouts, acquiring companies often become so burdened with debt that they have to concentrate on repaying it rather than on business investment that, in the long run, might prove crucial to their survival.

THE 'NEW' CAPITALISM

What we observe is a complex world which operates in a very different manner from the world observed by Adam Smith, or even Alfred Marshall. First, it is a world of bigness. Capitalists no longer act independently, but in concert, through the bureaucracies of complex organizations. Second, ownership patterns are markedly different from the eighteenth-or nineteenth-century theoretical views. The capitalist and the labouring classes are substantially blurred in modern societies. In the United States, roughly half of the common shares traded on the New York Stock Exchange are controlled by pension funds and similar trusts. It is not just the welfare of 'moguls' which these funds optimize, but the welfare of workers and business people who are planning for financial security and retirement.

Ownership rights to contemporary corporations are traded in massive volumes in sophisticated markets. Common stock is an indirect ownership claim upon corporate capital. Although contemporary products of the financial services industry are diverse, finance generally differs from common stock as follows: it pays a fixed rate of return; it stands ahead of 'common' in the event of default; and it is issued as a liability rather than as an equity.

Automation makes it possible for large and small traders to participate in trading. Markets presumably offer the same efficient service to the trader of a few shares, as an institutional trader receives. Of course, market sophistication is not limited to trading in equities. Markets for financial instruments abound, and international trading in equities and finance is also commonplace. Actual transactions probably occur at remote locations, and may be reported only moments later to a broker or other financial intermediary, possibly thousands of miles from the market. Certainly the milieu of contemporary capitalism is strikingly different from the technological vision embodied in the neoclassical system.

A third characteristic of modern capitalism is related to the other two. It is risk-spreading, or diversification. It is possible for a single transactor to hold pieces, or shares of many different enterprises, simultaneously. And, regardless of the number of the shares, it is quite feasible for the transactor to move with a minimum of obstacle and transaction cost, in a very fluid manner, between and among equities or financial assets.

Fourth, and finally, we identify as a characteristic of capitalism the manner in which its denizens are trained. Contemporary business education is strongly focused upon imparting financial management skills. Financial optimization is the vanguard of contemporary business education. Students learn rate-of-return analysis as the omnipresent reality.

RATE OF RETURN ANALYSIS

The utility-maximizing transactor in the conventional business learning model chooses among alternatives for the placement of wealth. In sophisticated markets wealth placements may be shifted virtually continuously. Such is the strategy of the savvy transactor who may strive to 'keep all options open' on a continuing basis.

The opportunity cost of placing wealth in asset B is the income forgone, due to choosing the lesser valued asset, when the highest valued asset, A, could have been chosen instead. To minimize the opportunity cost associated with any choice, then, the rational transactor will strive to make ongoing wealth placements so that the *ex post* rate of return on all placements is revealed to be equal to the highest risk-adjusted rate that is paid to the most attractive placement. Information on the attractiveness of placements is provided by the dissemination of *ex post* market trading information.

Following the dicta of contemporary managerial finance is the rational means by which individual transactors can enhance their wealth positions. But we must also ask if the prescription that benefits a single transactor also benefits the whole of society. Could it be possible, for instance, that a tragedy of the commons may be implicit in the manner in which the denizens of financial management are trained? If so, then we might expect to see a rather interesting anomaly of modern management education. That anomaly would be a negative correlation between the number of managers so trained in managerial finance, and aggregate economic performance. As the number of managers increases, an extant economy might actually experience a weakening, or even a decline in its vitality.

CURIOUSM

We have used the term 'curiousm' to mean an anomaly, which is an irregularity or deviation from the common rule. The quest at hand is to explain how the pursuit of the dicta of the conventional theory – the practice of financial management – could actually provoke a tragedy of the commons. Specifically, our intent is to demonstrate how it might be possible for individual optimizing behaviour to result in a societal outcome in which the economic welfare of the whole may not be maximized. In fact, we shall describe how the pursuit of the optimizing dicta of the conventional wisdom may result in the attainment of the stationary state with zero growth, or even a state in which society's stock of wealth is actually declining.

Recall Table 6.1. The optimizing dicta of the neoclassical theory specifies that the capitalist should hire units of variable input labour up to that point at which marginal revenue product is equal to marginal factor cost. By using a MFC of $5 and a product price of $2 in this example, we see that the rational capitalist hires five workers, produces twenty-five units of output per period, and earns a total profit of $25. The addition to profit associated with hiring the first worker is $9. For the second through the fifth workers it is $7, $5, $3, and $1 respectively.

Now, suppose we shift from nineteenth-century Marshallian capitalism to observe the contemporary milieu in which a typical firm sets its rates of output and employment. For instance, if this capitalist hired only four workers, produced twenty-two units of output and earned

$24 of quasi-rent, we should want to know why he apparently suboptimizes output and employment, rather than acting in accord with the dicta of the neoclassical theory.

Suppose that the firm is operated in a manner indicative of the new capitalism. That is, let us suppose that the capitalist is acquired by a large conglomerate which trades freely in subsidiary enterprises, by buying and selling them. In this environment the profit-maximizing goal of the conglomerate parent may be very different from its subsidiaries, if they operated independently instead. Whereas the subsidiary or capitalist optimizes by conserving its fixed inputs which are typically tangible capital assets, the conglomerate optimizes by conserving the scarcity of financial assets.

TOTAL PROFIT VERSUS. PROFIT RATE

The data in Table 6.1, through column 6, are reproduced in Table 8.1. From the conglomerate's point of view, it seeks to allocate budget to each of its subsidiaries so as to maximize the rate of return on its scarce resource, which is finance. At the margin, then, the conglomerate is interested in minimizing the opportunity cost of its financial placement (budget) with the subsidiary capitalist in this example. Analysis suggests the possibility of reallocating the amount of finance necessary to support the last worker – number 5 – to another subsidiary where it might earn a higher rate of return.

Clearly, any decision to cut variable input below five workers is suboptimal in the Marshallian system. But the Marshallian convention, as it is taught to sophomore economics students, considers only the value of real inputs like labour and capital. Financial costs are omitted. When the cost of finance is considered, we shall see that it has a profound impact upon prescriptive optimizing behaviour.

If the conglomerate assigns an opportunity cost of 25 per cent to the budgeted finance costs supporting the fifth worker, the subsidiary must earn that marginal rate in order to retain that worker. For instance, we shall assume that the maintenance of each worker requires a continuous financial outlay of $200. At 25 per cent, then, the cost of finance to support a worker is $50, which we round to $1 per period, or week. This raises marginal factor cost from $5, to $6 in column 7 of Table 8.1. Now the marginal product of the fifth worker is three units, and these are sold for $2 each, for a total of $6. Since financial costs raise MFC, worker number 5 becomes a break-even

Table 8.1   Hourly production, cost and revenue data

1 Units of variable input	2 Total product	3 Marginal product	4 Product price	5 Total revenue	6 Marginal revenue product	7 MFC *	8 MFC **
1	7	7	$2	$14	$14	$6	$9
2	13	6	2	26	12	6	9
3	18	5	2	36	10	6	9
4	22	4	2	44	8	6	9
5	25	3	2	50	6	6	9
6	27	2	2	54	4	6	9
7	28	1	2	56	2	6	9

*   Assumes 25 per cent opportunity cost of finance
** Assumes 100 per cent opportunity cost of finance

alternative and is therefore no longer profitable. Profitability for the subsidiary now begins with the employment of the fourth worker. Further, if the opportunity cost of finance increases to 100 per cent, then MFC increases to $9 (see column 8). At that required rate of return, worker number 4 becomes unprofitable, since his marginal revenue product of $8 is exceeded by his marginal factor cost of $9.

The motivation of the parent conglomerate is not to obtain the maximization of total profit on the fixed capital assets of each of its subsidiaries. From the conglomerate's perspective, the scarce resource to be conserved is its own scarce stock of finance. Note the apparent loss to society of output and jobs. This presents no problem if the assumption of perfect competition is fulfilled. Freedom of entry and exit should attract new firms to the industry, so long as profits exist. However, a substantial problem becomes apparent if any degree of power is exercised in output markets. For instance, if entry conditions in an industry can be limited, then the total number of firms in that industry could be constrained and societal output and employment would therefore be rendered suboptimal.

Since the conglomerate exercises market power as the sole 'buyer' of financial placements from its subsidiary providers, it is motivated to manipulate its subsidiaries so as to maximize the average rate of return on its aggregate stock of finance. To the extent that the rate of return on a marginal dollar of finance placed with a subsidiary slips below the average rate of return for the conglomerate's aggregate stock of finance, the parent will minimize opportunity cost by reallocating finance away from that subsidiary to other uses. In doing so the marginal rate of return on the subsidiary's budget may come to approach the average rate for the entire conglomerate.

CAPITAL DECONSERVATION

In the Marshallian system the capitalist conserves his fixed asset by maximizing quasi-rent, which controls the intensity of variable input usage. Maximization of quasi-rent is compatible with maximization of total profit. Output is added, and also units of variable input, even though the average product of the variable input, and therefore the average rate of return on the fixed asset, is falling. Maximization of total profit is compatible with a declining rate of profitability, or average profit on the fixed asset.

Recall that in the neoclassical world of Alfred Marshall capitalists act individually rather than in concert through complex organizations, that they are required to acquire and to hold assets to fruition, and that they are required to hold them in their entirety. The contemporary conglomerate presents a very different illustration. We have carefully observed the neoclassical profit lacuna in Chapter 7 and we have acknowledged that it may lead to a blurring of the distinction between profit and interest, and therefore to a blurring of capital and rentier assets. We are now able to consider how the pursuit of the optimizing dicta of the neoclassical theory may lead a contemporary firm to 'deconservation' or to the disinvestment of its capital.

In our illustration of the conglomerate, capital deconservation may occur as a conglomerate parent acquires subsidiaries and then operates them at rates of output and employment that are suboptimal according to the basic Marshallian dicta. This variance occurs because of fundamental differences in the objectives of the capitalist's productive unit, and the objectives of the conglomerate. Whereas the former is motivated to conserve capital assets in order to earn maximum total profit, the latter is motivated to conserve its aggregate stock of finance by maximizing the overall rate of return.

INDUSTRIAL ORGANIZATION

Proponents of maintaining the status quo in American industry typically argue that mergers, acquisitions, buy-backs, and other financial manipulations by corporations are indications of healthy competition, and not a cause for alarm. Freeing American corporations from antitrust laws has been advocated in some quarters, including the Reagan administration. Frequently business advocates point to limited evidence of growing industrial concentration. There generally exists no evidence that key American industries are substantially more 'monopolized' or 'oligopolized' as the result of contemporary corporate financial practices, than a few decades ago.

But looking only at monopolization in output markets begs the question of possible detrimental effects from finance-motivated ownership. To the extent that finance-motivated organizations can force their subsidiaries to deconserve their fixed capital assets, then the problem goes far beyond concern over output market power and price control. Instead, the contemporary policy issue pertains to the inefficient use of societal resources by corporations.

Recall that the first glitch of capitalism is disequilibrium hoarding. Some portion of saving may be committed to non-productive, or rentier use. The outcome is a declining level of output and employment. The public policy solution to hoarding goes beyond Keynes's prescription that government must provide the extra investment necessary to close the recessionary gap. The prescription of disequilibrium analysis is more precise. It requires government to implement disincentives to stop the conversion of current saving or prior accumulation into non-productive use.

The second glitch of economic theory is the profit lacuna. Because the neoclassical synthesis lacks a theory of profit, transactors who pursue its dicta in a complex economy are led to treat capital homogeneously with finance. This blurring of the distinction between profit and interest is an outcome of the neoclassical synthesis which specifies that the reward to capital and other assets is only the reward of waiting to consume. Related to the neoclassical view of capital is the marginal productivity theory of distribution. It decrees that an extra dollar of any economic resource should earn the same rate of return as an extra dollar of any other resource.

Conventional practices of corporate financial management typically lead to the conservation of finance, rather than to the conservation of tangible capital. The typical conglomerate seeks to earn the same risk-adjusted rate of return on its marginal placements of finance, as it earns on any other placements of finance in the firm's most highly valued use. By shifting finance continuously among subsidiaries, by buying and selling subsidiaries, and also by seeking alternative placements for finance outside the parent firm, the conglomerate may possibly attain a constant, high-valued rate of return on every dollar of finance placed.

Risk can be valued in a sophisticated market environment. But entrepreneur characteristics of skill and industry are more subjective, and less easily valued in the market place. To the extent that wealth can be committed to some non-productive use at the 'going' market rate of return, without proffering skill and industry, then it is in the transactor's best interest to navigate the 'low path'. Savvy transactors are likely to reward assets only for the value of waiting, and for risk, and to avoid holding assets which require additional compensation for the skill and industry of the entrepreneur. The consequence may be that assets with demonstrative industry and skill components associated with their use may be neglected in favour of assets which do not require the compensation of those components.

CAPITAL SHORTAGE

Capital shortage is the outcome of the second glitch of capitalism. As in the illustration of the conglomerate, the capital assets of subsidiaries may be underutilized and therefore subject to deconservation. In the limiting case, society may reduce net investment until it ultimately attains the vision of the neoclassical world, which is the stationary state. Here, saving is just equal to depreciation and net investment is zero. The class of capitalists becomes a class of rentiers, since they are neither motivated nor rewarded for providing skill and industry. Growth ceases. Wealth accumulation occurs for any individual or group of individuals in stationary society, only at the cost of some other individual or group that forfeits its wealth position. In stationary society, the attainment and retention of wealth is a zero sum game.

This translates into the failure of the private or non-profit organization to obtain the short run. Recall that profit and economic growth occur exclusively in Marshall's short period. The long period is a planning horizon, in which investment and growth do not occur. Profit is zero in the competitive long run.

We might ask, then, what may be the outcome if the contemporary organization remains perpetually in the long run and fails to engage the short run? It might do so by holding finance rather than capital assets, or by converting capital assets to nonproductive rentier use. To the extent that the corporation may keep its options perpetually open, the short run in which tangible capital assets are conserved may never be attained. The corporation would be compensated as a rentier or financier only, which is the compensation for waiting. Risk would be compensated. But skill and industry would not be compensated, since they receive their profit reward in the short run as a consequence of asset conservation.

Perpetual avoidance of the short run by the contemporary, complex organization may be expedient for an isolated transactor. But if this behaviour becomes adopted as the 'best practice' management strategy, then a tragedy of the commons results. The commonweal is no longer benefited as an outcome of economic actions motivated solely by self-interest.

CAPITAL AND THE COMMONWEAL

Capital in Ricardo's system is very apparent. It is seed corn committed to the ground. And it is differentiated in its use from grain of identical quality which is used for consumption, or as a rentier asset. Grain which is used as capital must be used productively: that is, it must be committed to the ground with skill and industry, and in an environment of risk.

Contemporary capital is more amorphous in nature than Ricardian capital, and it is therefore much more difficult to specify. In a monetary economy with sophisticated markets for equity and finance, the nature of capital can be quite obscure. Shifting from an agricultural or industrial economic base, to an economy based upon information and services, further intensifies this obscurity.

The decrees of government, and externalities, add significantly to the capital specification problem. Some production activities become outlawed, and are therefore non-productive. The 'underground' production and sale of marijuana and other drugs is an illustration. It may be the will of society that agricultural land be used productively for the cultivation of grain, instead of for growing marijuana, for instance. But to the extent that the law can be subverted, then land and other resources may shift from productive to non-productive use.

An externality is the conferral of a cost or a benefit, associated with consumption or production, which cannot be assigned through the market system. Pollution is often sighted as an example of a negative externality. Producers may degrade environmental quality in creating their products. But neither producers nor consumers may be required to compensate society for the costs of restoring the environment to its original condition, unless government intervenes and levies charges in the form of effluent fees or other taxes.

CAPITAL AND METAPHYSICS

What we point out, of course, is that there may not be perfect articulation between what society chooses to produce and to officially count as part of gross national product, and what private transactors actually produce and consume. This may lead to a disparity between the definition of socially necessary capital for production, and those non-productively used assets which are rewarded illegitimately as capital goods.

When society specifies what it will count and what it will exclude from GNP, it is implicitly defining legitimate economic output. And by defining output, it simultaneously delineates the composition of capital necessary to produce that output. As such, capital becomes less of a technically specified resource, and therefore it becomes more of a metaphysical good. It is defined as capital by collective choice. Metaphysics is used here, in the sense of being marked by elaborate subtleties of thought or expression in the capital selection process.

Capital does not exist in a stationary society in which rentiers and financiers control all assets, and society is just satisfied to perpetuate the composition of current output. The absence of profit is a special case in Ricardo's system, wherein all capitalists become reduced to rentiers or financiers. In that system, capital is required to change the wealth position of society. In complex society – even a complex stationary society – capital is required to create change. And it is essential to any change from the status quo, compared to the outcome that would result if the status quo carries forward to fruition. We therefore define capital in a complex society as assets or resources that are necessary to change the character of society.

This argument supports the claim that a capital shortage exists in the United States and other mature capitalist economies. This shortage is manifested in a decline in favourable economic outcomes. Opponents may assert that the essential quantity of capital is an empirical proposition that can be technically specified. Since capital can be aggregated and counted, any long-term shortage could only exist in the presence of market power, wherein a price above the competitive equilibrium would call forth a constrained quantity.

But in Walras and in Ricardo, capital is not an aggregate stock, so much as it is a set of assets that are committed to productive use. In complex society with externalities and legally sanctioned activities, the definition of productive use cannot be supplied by the market alone. It must be specified by non-market collective choice. Government enforces that choice through regulatory, tax and other incentives and disincentives.

It may be argued that there is no problem with the proliferation of finance, so long as finance is channelled to some ultimate capital placement. But if finance is perceived as an economic activity, then it generates both output and income. While it is true that the proliferation of financial output may ultimately benefit capital placement, the proliferation of income from financial activities is a claim on society's output. To the extent that income from finance may be rising as a proportion of total income, then it is quite legitimate to assert a value that too large a portion of national output is being claimed by individuals pursuing finance-motivated activities.

'QUANTUM THEORY' OF CAPITAL

Some similarities exist between economics and physics with regard to qualifications of the assumptions underlying the classical world. Classical physics at the hand of Isaac Newton was mechanistic and deterministic. Cartesian reductionism decrees that the world is like a machine, and that it can be known by separating it into parts, and then can be obtained by aggregating the parts back into the whole. In the classical realm the world is objective and therefore it exists independently of the observer.

Quantum mechanics, on the other hand, rejects the determinism of Newtonian mechanics and offers in its place a more plausible explanation of submolecular activity. Instead, it asserts that reality at this level is 'symbiotic'. The observer participates with the observed and therefore affects the outcome. By watching, then, the outcome is made different than if the event had occurred in isolation, or if the observation was in some other way unique.

Like physics, conventional economics is also based upon a classical world view. But unlike the physicists, economists have not effectively grappled with the limiting power of the classical metaphor as it may be confronted by time and friction in an extant economy. A non-deterministic view of economics, like quantum mechanics in physics, should allow for interaction between the observer and the observed. A non-deterministic, non-objective view of the capital component of the *laissez-faire* doctrine should therefore reject capital as a technically specified quantity. Rather, its analogous treatment should allow for its subjective specification through non-market collective choice.

HOARDING FINANCE

Since capital in a complex society is related to changing states of that society, it is entirely possible that too many assets may be held in non-productive use. Simultaneously, there may exist a shortage of productively held assets, relative to some dynamic scenario which society may choose for some future period. A capital shortage, then, need not be defined as an aggregate shortage of assets. Rather, it may be a shortage of a particular kind of assets, held in productive use.

This capital shortage hypothesis is also associated with the claim that society has created too large a stock of rentier and financier assets. For instance, it may be claimed that too large a portion of society's transactions are financial in nature. Opponents of the claim may argue that the quantity of financial transactions, relative to the quantity of transactions involving final output, is technically specified. Some optimum quantity of financial transactions can be related to some optimum quantity of GNP. Also, finance is a service, and in a service-oriented economy it will be increasingly represented as a 'final' consumption good. If consumers choose it at its offering price, then it should not be considered to be over-supplied.

But just as the composition of capital may be specified metaphysically rather than technically, so also must the nature of capital be specified by non-market collective choice. Again, the distinction between the simplistic Ricardian world, and the complexity of our own, is that all output is not equally valued by society. Finance and rent are but payments to maintain the status quo by maintaining assets in their present use. Change, on the other hand, requires a different set of assets. To accomplish change, asset-holders must be compensated for the risk, skill and industry implicit in obtaining the divergent outcome.

LEARNING BY DOING

The Learning by Doing Hypothesis is associated with Nobel laureate Kenneth Arrow. It captures the effects of the 'learning curve' in a production setting. In the Marshallian short period we would expect labour productivity to increase dramatically in a relatively short period, following the installation of a capital asset. New technology may be 'embodied' in the asset. Workers who use it are therefore rendered more productive than if they had continued to work with an outdated one. The learning curve quickly begins to flatten out following the initial acquaintance of workers with capital. But beyond the initial surge of productivity, a longer range productivity effect is also observed. In fact, labour productivity may be a long-lived phenomenon, even when the asset continues unchanged. The production team simply becomes more proficient, often year after year, as tasks become standardized, coordination is improved, and production systems are refined.

Learning by doing is an outcome of stability of the productive environment. Devendra Sahal (1981) points out that growth-stimulating technical advances invariably depend upon the accumulation of production experience, which is dependent upon a stable production environment. In a study of the Swedish steelworks at Horndal, E. Lundberg (1961) reported an annual rate of growth in output per person hour of about 2 per cent per year over a fifteen-year period. Lundberg attributed the outcome entirely to learning by doing, since it occurred during a period in which no change took place in production technology, and no further investment was made in the facility. A similar outcome is also cited by P. A. David (1975). For twenty-two years following the construction of one of the production facilities at the Lawrence (Mass.) Textile Mill, new investment was essentially zero except for maintenance and repair work. Nevertheless, the productivity of the plant (measured in cloth yardage per person hour) continued to increase at an average annual rate of about 2.25 per cent during the period of study. In both cases, productivity improvement was attributed entirely to human learning that accrued to the acquisition of practical know-how in a stable environment.

Productivity improvement is the most significant source of economic growth. The learning by doing hypothesis therefore offers substantial insight into sources and causes of economic growth. Productivity improvement that accrues to learning by doing may be portrayed as quasi-rent in the Marshallian short-period model. Its fruits are the outcome of conservation of the fixed asset, which in these examples, is specified as plant and equipment.

The goal of any chief executive officer (CEO) of a contemporary corporation is to maximise in each calendar quarter the rate of return on the wealth placements of shareholders. Earlier in this chapter we have described how a modern organization could be motivated to reject the Marshallian short run, and to remain perpetually in the long run in which its options for the rearrangement of its wealth position are never foreclosed. To the extent that the contemporary organization may be motivated to maximize the rate of return on the aggregate stock of its finance, rather than to maximize total profit associated with individual assets, then disinvestment is a likely outcome. Assets and subsidiaries may be bought, sold or liquidated in order to provide a high financial rate of return for the financially motivated owner.

This finance-motivated strategy does not stabilize the capitalistic productive unit. Instead, it destabilizes it by motivating output and employment decisions that are irrational from the perspective of asset conservation. Managers may be transferred, workers may be laid off, and assets may by reassigned or even terminated without regard for the long-lived productivity outcome. The result of such a financial-oriented style of management may be disinvestment and therefore the organization may fail to obtain the benefits of human learning that only accrue to stability of the productive environment.

SOLVING THE SECOND GLITCH

Recall that the first glitch of economic theory is the failure of the conventional wisdom to account for disequilibrium hoarding. The Keynesian prescription for economic gluts requires that the government make up the difference between the amount of investment that may be forthcoming, and the amount of investment that would be forthcoming at full employment. The disequilibrium prescription described herein is more focused than the Keynesian prescription. Economic gluts may be resolved by the form of government intervention prescribed by the Keynesians. But they can be resolved more efficiently by quelling disequilibrium hoarding. In the 1970s this might have been revealed as a differential tax on income derived from the speculative sale of real estate, *objets d'art*, etc. In the period of high interest rates that prevailed at the beginning of this decade, it might have been revealed as a differential tax on income derived from holding interest-bearing finance.

Beyond hoarding, the second glitch is particularly appropriate to understanding organizational hoarding behaviours of the 1970s and 1980s. As such, it provides an explanation for the low-growth dysfunction of the post-Vietnam War period. The contemporary period is unlike the Great Depression, which was an economic glut. Contemporary problems have revealed themselves to be growth and supply oriented, rather than consumption and demand oriented.

The second glitch of economic theory portrays a particular kind of disequilibrium hoarding behaviour. Particularly large organizations may be motivated to hoard by shifting capital assets from productive to non-productive use. Like the first glitch, the principle solution to the second glitch is for government to provide disincentives to disinvestment. So, with regard to the role of government, the two glitches of capitalism may be resolved by the following actions. For the first glitch, a tax or sanction can be placed on hoarding behaviour. The second glitch can also be resolved by appeal to tax or sanction, but these must be precisely formulated to overcome the profit lacuna. The rate of profit on capital must be specified. And before that can occur, collective action must be taken to resolve the question of what constitutes capital in contemporary society.

Part V

Public Policy

The ultimate focus of this book is public policy. It considers the linkage between economic theory and the application of the conventional wisdom through the practice of economic policy. Its principal thesis is that contemporary economic problems should not be addressed merely on an *ad hoc* basis. There is a larger pattern evident in the character of economic dysfunction.

The legitimate role of government in remedying economic dysfunction is the object of Chapter 9. *Laissez-faire* is discarded in exchange for a 'mixed capitalist' system in which government plays two roles *vis-à-vis* the private sector. First, it is government's needful responsibility in a free, contemporary capitalist society to remedy any private sector investment shortfall. This is the Keynesian prescription. Government should also regulate hoarding activity which transfers assets from productive to non-productive use. Second, government must go beyond the Keynesian prescription to specify, through non-market collective action, what the composition of capital should be.

Chapter 10 addresses the unavoidable disintegration of international free trade as a consequence of responding to the second glitch of economic theory. In Chapter 11, 'Reaganomics', it is argued that supply side policies are none other than the *laissez-faire* resurgence. These are doomed to failure because they do not recognize the necessity that the composition of capital goods chosen by society can no longer be determined efficiently by the private sector.

9 What Is the Legitimate Role of Government?

Keynes pointed out in Chapter 12 of *The General Theory* that investments which are 'fixed' for the community are thus made 'liquid' for the individual. Transactors too often concentrate their efforts on liquidity, rather than productivity. 'The actual, private object of the most skilled investment to-day,' according to Keynes, 'is "to beat the gun" . . . to outwit the crowd, and to pass the bad, or depreciating, half-crown to the other fellow.' Such transfers of assets, according to Keynes, are 'a game of Snap, of Old Maid, of Musical Chairs – a pastime in which he is victor who says snap neither too soon nor too late, who passes the Old Maid to his neighbor before the game is over, who secures a chair for himself when the music stops'.

Unfortunately, as Keynes pointed out, there is no clear evidence that profitable investment policy for the individual is also advantageous for society. Investment, from society's perspective, 'needs more intelligence to defeat the forces of time and our ignorance of the future'. The goal of investment policy in capitalist societies should be to make more permanent the linkage between capital and capitalist. Said he:

> The spectacle of modern investment markets has sometimes moved me toward the conclusion that to make the purchase of an investment permanent and indissoluble, like marriage, except by reason of death or other grave cause, might be a useful remedy for our contemporary evils. For this would force the investor to direct his mind to the long-term prospects and to those only.

According to the terminology we have used, Keynes's argument is akin to requiring the asset-holder to engage the capital asset throughout the Marshallian short period. A means by which this might be accomplished, according to Keynes, is: 'The introduction of a substantial government transfer tax on all transactions . . . with a view to mitigating the predominance of speculation over enterprise in the United States.'

Lord Keynes supported the proposition that capital assets could also be financed publicly, rather than privately. Public investment, he

125

said, could overcome the greed-motivated tendency to transfer assets unpropitiously through the medium of finance. We shall argue, however, that it is possible to retain private title to capital assets while overcoming the destabilizing effects of non-productive finance, and without necessitating public financing. This can be accomplished through the specialized application of Keynes's 'transfer tax' which is implemented through a process of indicative economic planning.

THE APPROPRIATE GOVERNMENT ROLE

In an actual economy, some combination of appropriate government spending and government regulation of hoarding activity is necessary to maintain full employment. But this is not all. The second glitch of capitalism is the profit lacuna. In a complex economy, it is manifested by a blurring of the distinction between capital and rentier assets. The consequence is a capital shortfall, and possibly the attainment of the stationary state. To overcome this second glitch, an additional role for government is specified. That is, beyond investment stimulation and the regulation of hoarding, government must also specify what the rate of profit on capital goods shall be.

Since contemporary capital is not a homogeneous good, an aggregate quantity cannot be technically specified. So the rate of profit cannot be set by government action until the nature of capital goods is specified by collective action. This first requires a description of the composition and quantity of output desired by society to be obtained in the future. The difference between future output desired by society, and the composition and quantity of output that would emerge from a forward extension of the status quo, is the character of output for which government intervention is intended. Capital, then, is the stock of productive goods and services that is essential to obtaining the output differential between what is wanted and what would be produced without intervention. More abstractly, capital is essential to obtaining some future outcome for society, in contrast with the outcome that would be revealed without such government intervention.

It is asserted that the determination of what the composition and quantity of future output should be, the identification of capital goods necessary to obtain that end, and the specification of the rate of profit on each type of capital essential to call forth that quantity through private markets, should be taken by collective rather than market action. It is called indicative economic planning. The object of such planning in contemporary society is to overcome the second glitch of capitalism. In order to implement it, the rate of profit on various classes of capital goods must be regulated by government. Doing so is akin to imposing a transfer tax, as suggested by Keynes, in order to 'make indissoluble' the relationship between capital and investor.

INDICATIVE ECONOMIC PLANNING

Indicative economic planning is the strategy by which Japan has gained economic leadership of the free world. Robert Ozaki (1984) points out that Japan's version of economic planning is an alternative to forms practised by communist states, socialist or fascist states, or Western capitalist democracies such as the United States.

> It is not of a dictatorial, coercive sort, but rather is meant to indicate or anticipate the forthcoming major developments that will affect the nation's economy and to help make necessary adjustments as soon and as smoothly as possible. Based on analysis of hard data, it adds an element of certainty, continuity, and consistency to the nation's economic policy. It is a case of programming for dynamic growth of a competitive economy; planning is thus an instrument of pragmatism devoid of socialist ideological content.

Ozaki continues by pointing out that the United States in the post-Second World War era has based its economic progress upon the neoclassical synthesis which prescribes government management through a mix of monetary and fiscal policies sufficient to generate adequate aggregate demand. He says that the problem with the doctrine is that it is primarily meant to cope with the problems of short-run business fluctuations. It assumes, he says, that a long run is but a succession of short runs, and that if the economy is properly managed today, it will grow on its own 'over the long haul'. This assumption seemed to work up to the mid-1960s, he says, but not thereafter.

Japan adopted capitalism from the West in the nineteenth century. Embedded therein was the Western ideology of individualism and economic freedom. Ozaki points out that the notion that the state and the individual necessarily form an adversarial relationship is anathema to the Japanese concept of the nation-family. So also is the Japanese commitment to economic ideology. Like West Germany, Japan's economy was reborn from the ashes of the Second World War. It was pragmatism, and not ideology, that was the visïon of Japanese economic development. Necessity truly was the mother of invention. The Japanese have been unobligatory about carrying forward the 'excess baggage' of the conventional economic wisdom. If it works, an idea is used. If it does not, it is discarded.

Central to the Japanese method of indicative economic planning is what Ozaki calls 'vision-making'. It is undertaken by an agency of the Japanese Government called the Ministry of International Trade and Industry (MITI). Represented on 'deliberation councils' of MITI are participants from big and small business, government, consumers, academia, mass media, labour and local interest groups. The goal of these councils is to formulate a vision of what lies ahead.

> Specifically, the council is charged with the task of identifying the nature and direction of changes taking place in the overall econ-omic environment, determining what sort of new industrial struc-ture is most desirable for the nation, and indicating what are the most effective policy means to carry out the desired structural transformation of industry, and how and where those means should be applied.
>
> The 'vision' that results from council deliberations is published and widely circulated in the nation. Vision-making is the Japanese version of indicative economic planning, intended to build a con-sensus among all segments of society concerning the country's industrial structure, to ensure continuity and stability. (Ozaki, 1984)

An American version of indicative economic planning would prob-ably be somewhat more focused upon domestic output, relative to producing for foreign markets. In arriving at consensus, two major differences are apparent between Japan and the United States. The first is the uniquely international character of the Japanese process. Since such a significant part of Japan's economy is geared for export, MITI embodies a special commitment to export industries. An American version of indicative economic planning would probably be somewhat more focused upon domestic output relative to production for foreign markets. And second, Japan is a consensus society. The processes that operate in public decision-making in Japan are very different from those which operate in American society, where independent action is favoured. This is not to say that indicative economic planning cannot work in the United States, but only that the process would be less intuitive and therefore more costly and difficult for the American people to implement.

THE JAPANESE MYSTIQUE

Something more needs to be said about MITI and how it works in the Japanese economy. Ozaki points out that economic planning is associated only indirectly with industrial policy. The 'alternate scenarios' drafted by deliberation councils bear little similarity to the five-year plans of Soviet-style command economies. At most, says Ozaki, the plans indicate what the government is thinking, about the direction in which the economy is moving, and the problems it may be facing. Information provided in the planning process is useful to both private firms and public or non-profit organizations. However, the plans in no way obligate the private sector to proceed in the prescribed manner.

MITI's powers are substantially weaker than in earlier decades immediately following the Second World War. MITI cannot conveniently dictate or persuade businesses to act in the name of national interest. Cooperation is a matter of individual discretion. Even so, the nature of government–business consensus in Japanese society is conciliatory, rather than adversarial, as in the United States. This tends to make the Japanese approach to economic planning indicative, indirect, soft-handed, small scale, and market-oriented.

A recent example pertains to the so-called 'fifth-generation' or artificial intelligence supercomputer project (1982–91). The project has been 'spear-headed' by a 100 billion yen government industry consortium that includes eight leading producers. The goal, of course, is to set a precedent for a Japanese breakaway from the pattern of following US computer technology.

The success of the Japanese economy in the post-Second World War era is widely acknowledged and needs no documentation here. But perhaps we should pause briefly to marvel at the Japanese 'miracle', as did the *San Diego Union* in an editorial on 14 August 1985. (On that date the writer happened to be at Disneyland with his 11-year-old son.) Forty years ago today, the editorial reminded, Japan's attempt to carve out an empire in East Asia by force of arms collapsed in catastrophic defeat. Who could have dreamed at that time that Japan would lead the world economically in four short decades. The achievement is all the more remarkable given the dimensions of the Japanese defeat. It's major industries had been bombed into rubble. Most of its merchant fleet had been sunk. Japan had virtually no natural resources, and only one-sixth of the country was suitable for agriculture. Yet by 1952, the country had regained its pre-war levels of production. By the late 1970s, Japan's GNP exceeded that of France and Great Britain combined. Today, Japan is economically overtaking the Soviet Union. Industrial wages are now slightly higher than in the United States.

What is the reason for such a miracle, asks the *San Diego Union?* Some say it lies in the post-war aid Japan received from the United States ($2.4 billion). Others depict the Japanese as workaholic robots. Still others accuse Japan of growing rich through predatory trading practices, likened to a form of economic aggression.

Japan and the United States, of course, are dramatically different. Differences permeate culture styles, natural resource bases, land masses, and traditions, including intellectual traditions. In the late 1970s, as the American economy clearly began to manifest problems, it became popular for scholars and others to make the pilgrimage abroad to discover 'the Japanese mystique.' Numerous books and articles have bombarded the American intelligentsia, eulogizing one virtue or another discovered in the quest to improve American productivity and economic performance. The list includes quality circles, company unions, industrial robots, frugality, teamwork, and a host of others. But none of the specialized research 'sorties' has captured the deepest essence of what makes Japan work, in a general enough prescription that can be made applicable to the American economy. The *San Diego Union* gets very close to the matter, however, when it observes: 'The simple truth is that the Japanese . . . adopted . . . the one economic system capable of harnessing their one resource. The resource was the creative power of the Japanese people.'

CONSERVATION

America's long suit is surely in the quality of its human resources, particularly as we rush headlong into the information revolution. What is it about Japan's conservation of its 'people resource' that is so different from practices in the United States? The disinvestment thesis provides a clue to the new policy directions by which America may struggle to renew itself economically in the late twentieth century, in a manner analogous to Japan's renewal following the Second World War.

We have observed that Japan's pragmatic approach to economics makes it less tightly bound to the dicta of neoclassical economic theory. In Japan, economic performance is judged more broadly than from the vantage point of only the individual transactor. Private actions are more closely scrutinized for articulation with the common-weal than in the United States. In America, the tendency is to begin by assuming that self-interested action is innately compatible with collective action.

Japan's long suit is asset conservation, regardless of the dicta of conventional economic wisdom. Because of its dearth of land, Japan has always been forced to conserve scarce natural resources. Its economic infrastructure, developed in the capitalist mode after the Second World War, did so without adopting the Western convention of treating labour as the variable input. Instead, human capital was treated in the production schema as a societal asset, and therefore worthy of conservation, as scarce natural resources are worthy of conservation.

Human capital conservation policies in Japan have been well documented by American researchers over the past decade. Indeed, these practices are perhaps the greatest substance of what Americans perceive to be the Japanese mystique. The spectrum of human capital policies extends from quality circles, to 'lifetime employment' which affects about one quarter of the labour force, to enrichment policies which interconnect the workplace with the interpersonal lives of its workers.

Financial conservation policies are also apparent in the Japanese schema, and these can be compared and contrasted with American financial policies which are often asset-wasting. For instance, the typical Japanese firm is free of capitalist-owner control of management. Equity is typically held by banks rather than individual or institutional investors. Pressures to deliver attractive, market-rate performance at quarterly intervals are less severe. Long-term developmental strategies are generally more feasible in Japan because of ownership continuity. Since ownership is less likely to be transferred on the basis of quarterly financial performance, as in America, Japanese firms are better able to sustain short-term losses if they are ultimately followed by attractive pay-outs in the long term.

Walter E. Hoadley (1984) points out that financial markets and institutions are seldom free of government influence in all countries, including the United States and Japan. The difference between the two countries is that banking and financial policies are largely un-coordinated in America, whereas industry follows more directed policies and guidance procedures in Japan which are designed to further national objectives. In Japan, very strict rules were es-tablished after the Second World War to govern capital markets. The credit and tax systems were utilized heavily during the 1950s and 1960s to help specific industries and firms. Japanese financial regula-tions have been liberalized slowly in more recent years. One of the manifestations of government direction of financial markets is that interest rates are commonly negotiated in Japan, whereas in the United States they are set by market auction. An outcome of this system has been that Japanese companies have consistently benefited from somewhat lower costs of finance than their American counter-parts.

INDUSTRIAL POLICY

The contemporary interest in industrial policy is largely of Japanese origin. Its roots are in Japanese indicative economic planning. But at a higher level of abstraction, industrial policy can be defined as anything which the government does *vis-à-vis* the private sector. One might argue that it is the rationale for the presence of government in our mixed capitalist system which originated in the Great De-pression.

But the roots of government involvement in the American econ-omic system extend much further into our past. Government in-volvement in the economy was evident as early as 1862 with the passage of the Morrill Act creating land grant colleges. And it has been much more pervasive than is often portrayed. Certainly the GI Bill of 1944, the National Defense Highway Act of 1956, and the Defense Education Act of 1958 are cogent examples of American industrial policy intervention. With great interest, however, we ob-serve a convention that the American public appears uncomfortable with government intervention in the economy, except where it may be inspired or motivated by national defence considerations.

Aaron Wildavsky (1984), in a compendium on the industrial policy debate edited by Chalmers Johnson, points out that the term 'industrial policy' is a hotly contested concept in the United States. It means different things to different people. To some, it is an equity appeal for workers wounded by declining fortunes in manufacturing and other industries. To others it is an appeal for protectionism to shelter American industries and workers. Yet others see industrial policy as an agenda that supports capital modernization, regardless of the equity consequences.

Four different types of legislative proposals are identified by Wildavsky, although he points out that within each of the categories, the intent of various of the proposals and their advocates may be in diametric opposition to each other. First are credit proposals including various bills to establish a Reconstruction Finance Corporation that would grant loans or loan guarantees to individuals or companies otherwise unable to secure project financing.

Second are tax preferences. Wildavsky points out that anything that can be done by direct appropriations can also be accomplished indirectly through the use of tax preferences. Included herein are a variety of competing and often contradictory proposals such as the use of tax credits to induce employers to hire the long-term unemployed, to provide tax relief for businesses locating in 'enterprise zones', or even to treat dividends from cumulative preferred stock in the same way that interest on debt is now treated, as a tax deduction, to stimulate equity capital formation. The third class of legislative proposals addresses government regulations as diverse as curbing the 'runaway shop' from leaving the United States, to plant closing legislation, to selective nationalization. Proposal four advocates direct appropriations for a plethora of causes, including education and training, science and computer literacy, and physical 'infrastructure' redevelopment.

Ultimately, the industrial policy debate comes to rest upon the question of which 'stakeholders' get what favourable treatment, and for what purposes. Government intervention into the 'efficient market', of course, is tainted with possibilities for political pork-barrelling. Eugene Bardach (1984) argues that government agencies in the United States do not have a good record of accomplishing even medium-scale efforts at development assistance, much less very complex ones. He cities the Trade Readjustment Assistance Act of 1974, providing government relief to an injured class (workers unemployed by foreign competition), as an example of programmes with unlimited potential to suck up federal dollars.

Melvyn Krauss (1984) is perhaps even less sanguine. He observes that proponents of industrial policy in the United States aim to combine free trade with 'efficient subsidization'. But according to Krauss, equity and efficiency are incompatible in optimizing outcomes. We tend to agree.

The ultimate goal of any industrial policy must be economic growth, consistent and compatible with societal values. Equity protection of workers and other affected classes should not be the primary consideration of such policies. But if humane society is to exist, then a set of equity-oriented policies should protect the losers and the disenfranchised, and redistribute from the affluent to those who are less able to care with dignity for basic human needs. These values may coexist, and occasionally they may accommodate each other in the workplace, but very often they will be innately incompatible. All issues of justice cannot be resolved in the workplace. And a just society cannot allow such issues to remain unresolved.

TAX POLICIES

Economist Yolanda Henderson (1984) describes how tax reform is often advocated as an alternative to industrial policy, but it may actually be a component of industrial policy. The US tax system is already creating winners and losers among investment projects and industries. But the selection of who wins and who loses often occurs somewhat haphazardly, without an efficiency motive, and frequently as a consequence of political clout rather than concern for the commonweal.

Tax policy can encourage investment by taxing capital income at low rates. Also, it can encourage the efficient allocation of investment by specifying appropriate rates of tax on various projects. But the effect of taxes upon the economic growth outcome is often overlooked by policy-makers. Yet taxes play a critical role in choices between housing and industrial capital, between long-lived assets and short-lived equipment, between alternative industries such as cars or pharmaceuticals, or between the Sun Belt and the so called 'Rust Belt', and so on.

Actually, the US tax system produces high effective tax rates on some investments and very low rates, or even subsidies, on others. Wealth-holders are attracted to lightly taxed placements at the expense of highly taxed placements. The outcome can be 'inter-asset' or 'inter-sectorial' distortions. This tends to mask the real winners and losers among asset-holders.

Henderson argues that tax reform should focus upon creating a tax policy that is neutral towards various assets. The goal of such a policy, she argues, would be improved economic efficiency. We strongly disagree.

Tax policy can surely be an efficient vehicle for the implementation of indicative economic planning. Indeed, it can be used as the transfer tax suggested by Keynes to mitigate the predominance of speculation over productive enterprise. But whereas Henderson argues that the American tax system should be reformed to make it neutral across classes of assets, we argue that it should differentiate between capital assets and rentier and financier assets. Capital placements can be rewarded with subsidy (negative tax), or non-productive placements can be penalized by assessing a differential tax liability. A fundamental goal of tax policy should be to reward wealth placements that are tied to capital goods, and to penalize wealth placements that only serve rentier or financier consumption and therefore merely perpetuate the status quo.

Since the solution to the profit lacuna is to set the rate of profit exogenously, the first task of government through indicative economic planning should be to determine desired and feasible economic outcomes. These must be compared to the outcome that would result from an uninterrupted extension of the status quo. Government specification of the rate of profit, which is the solution to the profit lacuna, is translated through tax policy to provide a penalty for non-productive asset placements, relative to legitimate investment. Since rentiers and financiers pay higher tax rates on income received from non-productive asset holdings, there is incentive to increase the quantity of assets designated as capital, and to decrease the quantity of assets designated as non-productive. Tax policies, of course, are not the only means of implementing the rate of profit on capital. Direct regulation can also be used to mitigate speculation. Regulatory policies to limit corporate raids are examples of such policies.

LABOUR MARKET SHELTERS

Of particular concern to the implementation of indicative economic planning is the conservation of human capital, especially as America and her international competitors rush headlong through the information revolution. Surely, if America has a significant strength which distinguishes its workplace, it is in the quality of her human resources. Government has an important stake and responsibility in the conservation of America's human capital.

Internal labour markets are shelters for workers who are protected from entry level competition. Without them, workers would be forced to bid for their jobs continuously. Another benefit to employers of labour market shelters is the stability they provide in the productive environment. And stability can be an excellent source of productivity improvement through learning by doing.

Corporate raids often result in the destruction of labour market shelters. Some mergers are even undertaken to reduce unit labor costs through the dismantling of labour market shelters. To the extent that such practices may be non-productive, therefore resulting in disinvestment, they should be the objects of tax and regulatory intervention.

ADVERSARIAL RELATIONSHIPS

Whereas Japan's is a consensus society, America's is an adversarial one. And nowhere is the adversarial process more evident than at the nexus between business and government. The origins of this adversarial relationship have been carefully charted by Thomas K. McCraw (1984). He points out that the United States has an extremely small amount of state ownership of enterprise, in comparison with other developed countries. For instance, the United States is the only country besides South Korea with a completely private airline industry, the only country with an all-private telecommunications network, and one of only a few with no public enterprises in oil, gas and steel. The common perception that other governments tend to promote and to encourage the development of business enterprise while the United States tends to regulate and restrain it. according to McCraw, is generally an accurate perception. Despite numerous exceptions, says McCraw: 'There is little question that in cross-national comparison the United States does not promote business enterprise to the degree that its international competitors do or that the U.S. itself did earlier in its history.'

The rationale for business – government separatism is clear, upon appeal to our history. The United States was born into a conspicuous absence of established institutions. There existed no state church, no standing army, no hereditary aristocracy, and no clear locus of sovereignty. Instead, ours was to become an open, mobile society, protected from absolutism by the division of powers implicit in our Constitution. But as a consequence of the decisive actions of our founding fathers, a large portion of political and economic power was 'left up for grabs'.

Unlike other countries, the first powerful class to 'grab power' in the United States was the business class. One thinks of the decade of the 1880s, the meteoric rise of trusts, and of 'the robber barons' of that era. It wasn't until the Progressive Era (1901–14), according to McCraw, that Americans at large began to take a close and critical look at the impact of the abuses of business power which had developed in the vacuum. 'Progressive history told an exciting story. It recast the American experience as a continuous contest between public and private interests; that is to say, between right and wrong . . . Most of the evil was found to reside in the business community.'

In response, the Interstate Commerce Commission Act was passed in 1888, followed by the Sherman Anti-trust Act in 1890. Even so, it was in the first decade of this century that the adversarial relationship between business and government congealed. In the third decade, the 1920s, attacks on big business quieted down. But the advent of the Great Depression reconfirmed America's new-found view of business greed and abuse. By the middle of the twentieth century, the functional separateness of the public and the private sectors had become a mainstay of America's liberal creed. McCraw cities Arthur M. Schlesinger, Jr's books on Jacksonian Democracy and on the New Deal as evidence that 'Liberalism in America has been ordinarily the movement on the part of the other sections of society to restrain the power of the business community.'

ECONOMIC PLANNING

Economic planning is anathema to most Americans. Perhaps that repugnance stems from our historical distrust of bigness – not only in business, but also in government – and our adherence to *laissez-faire*. Aaron Wildavsky points out that the 'small is beautiful' movement is quintessentially American, particularly with regard to the relationship between business and government. During the Jacksonian era, roughly between the second and third decades of the nineteenth century, public opinion held that 'pure equality of opportunity would actually lead to substantial equality of results'. According to the Jacksonian position economic outcomes could be improved, 'If only the government would stop chartering banks, awarding franchises, forstering monopolies . . . and otherwise interfering with economic life.' Given the natural, rough equality of men, and bolstered by blessed American circumstances, the outcome would lead to as close an approximation of equality as human condition would allow. The belief of the Jacksonian era was that the pursuit of competitive individualism would lead to reasonably equal outcomes.

The contemporary manifestation of the Jacksonian view is the movement to get government off of the backs of the people. Less regulation is the spirit of the day. Reduction of government costs, even in the wake of deteriorating quality in human services and education, appears to be widely favoured by the American public. Somehow the belief persists that we are rooted in the prior successes of our *laissez-faire* tradition, that when other policies do not serve us well, we can and should retrench. This view is articulated in the contemporary manifestation of what we shall call the *laissez-faire* resurgence, or Reaganomics. We shall discuss Reaganomics at length in Chapter 11.

Economic planning is portrayed by advocates as indicative of big, wasteful and incompetent government. Surely the free market can make choices for the future more efficiently and effectively than the councils of government. Even prior to the landslide election of Ronald Reagan in 1980, widespread support existed for the deregulation of major industries including trucking, telecommunications, airlines and finance. Government intervention in business has been broadly viewed as a source of inefficiency and as an intuitive 'second best' behind the rationality of market action.

As Robert Clower (1974) has pointed out, Adam Smith espoused a system motivated by greed and controlled by a large number of uncoordinated agents, rather than the imposition of rules popularly perceived as arbitrary and oppressive. Adam Smith argued that *laissez-faire* could and should replace government direction and regulation in affairs of production and trade. What made his ideas so clever and cogent was his belief that the economic activities of countless individuals could best be coordinated by the impersonal action of 'natural market forces' through the exercise of competition and self-interest. Non-market public choice is anathema to doctrinaire *laissez-faire*.

Philosopher Karl Popper (1962) points out that *laissez-faire* fits within the class of ideological propositions which are innately incapable of being invalidated by science. Neither can science validate their rightness. To advocate myopically a return to *laissez-faire*, on the basis of a commitment to an eighteenth-century natural law doctrine, is both naive and cavalier. Complexity is an ever present reality of contemporary society. Modern science and technology ordains that we live in a world very different from that of Adam Smith. Complexity of the social structure leads to a default, rule-making role for government which can and should not be abandoned casually.

ENTROPY

A consideration of the second law of thermodynamics is useful here. Often it is referred to as the law of entropy. The term is ordinarily used to describe an outcome of advancing technology. Production transforms natural resources into forms of greater economic value than the form in which they existed in their primal states. But as economic value is added, resulting from specialized adaptation of the resource, the opportunity cost of using the residue and the scrap value, in some other productive process, also rises. Higher levels of production create more specialized residue and scrap, therefore embodying increasing amounts of entropy.

Petrochemicals, for instance, may be processed to more specialized and higher ordered uses, such as plastic. Ultimately, following its tenure of usefulness, the plastic becomes 'specialized garbage' which cannot be further operated upon with economic efficiency. Production processes thus raise resources from low entropy levels to high ones.

The entropy concept can also be applied to social systems. In this case we may think of processes or rules, rather than objects. In complex social systems, continuing challenge by the self-interested actions of individuals and special interest groups forces a system of rules to become more partitioned and specialized, and therefore to embody more entropy. The alternative to rule-making in complex and technology driven society is chaos and anarchy. Complex rules that are the ends of protracted processes of clarification and delineation may lead to societal stagnation, even to morbidity. The weight of a complex network of increasingly specialized rules may ultimately render the social system in which it operates unviable.

Our point is this. Competitive, self-serving transactors in a complex social system are likely to violate the commonweal, thereby invoking the tragedy of the commons. Technological sophistication in communications, transportation, etc., ordains the feasibility of such violations. Rule-making is the process by which government protects the commonweal from personal abuse. Even though it imposes a cost upon society, it is unrealistic to assume that the institution of the free market can resolve complexity in any humane way.

COLLECTIVE ACTION

It is ironic that the spirit of individualism that made America such a powerful economic force through the mid-twentieth century, now threatens its economic leadership. In *The Rise and Decline of Nations*, Mancur Olson (1982) argues that economists have paid insufficient attention to non-market groups and institutions which interfere with the economic activities of individuals. Contrary to arguments developed in earlier works, Olson now stresses the dark side of groups. Although these are often difficult to initiate, special interest groups or 'distributional coalitions' (unions, employers' groups, trade lobbies, etc.) can pursue their own interests which are often inimical to the commonweal. He argues that special interests seek ever larger slices of the economic pie for their members, even if the social costs are enormous. Further, once formed, special interest groups tend to persist, even if their initial usefulness is outgrown. They are, says Olson, the major reason why extant economies are not in equilibrium, why twentieth-century Great Britain has stagnated economically, and why cities in the Northeastern United States are decayed.

Contemporary America seems to exist on the horns of a perilous, even a cruel dilemma. The paradigm of rugged individualism is no longer operative. In the contemporary international milieu it is thoughtful collective action that is likely to advance the economic fortunes of nation states. Unfortunately, the tradition of collective action in the United States is not an attractive one. The past history of adversarial action between government and business does not bode optimistically for a brilliant future. Nor does America's experience with effectively initiating issues of non-market collective choice.

10 The Disintegration of the World Economy

Free trade means free from government intervention. Free international trade is exploding. From 8 per cent twenty-five years ago, it has grown to 16 per cent of the combined domestic products of international trading partners. For the United States alone it accounts for 14 per cent of GNP. By virtue of its size, the American economy is the world's largest exporter. This means that one out of every nine American jobs is in an export industry. And one in every seven GNP dollars is earned from sales to foreigners. On the import side, one of every four cars, 60 per cent of all televisions, 40 per cent of clothing and two-thirds of all shoes are produced outside the United States.

The economics of America's foreign trade are staggering. Not since 1971 has the United States run a surplus in its balance of trade account. In 1980, Americans imported 26 billion dollars more than we exported. But through the first half of 1986, the trade deficit was exploding at a rate of 159 billion dollars annually. And roughly one-third of this deficit is with a single country: Japan.

In 1985, for the first time since the First World War, America became a net debtor nation. This means that, on balance, Americans owe foreigners more than foreigners owe Americans. A manifestation of net debtor status is that foreigners are holding an increasing share of equity in American businesses, and in other domestic assets. It means the profit benefits to the ownership of American assets are increasingly accruing to foreign, rather than to American wealth placements.

Recent shock waves in Congress have fuelled the search for answers to explain the foreign trade deficit. Certainly, the numbers call into question America's future competitiveness in international markets. A recent *Wall Street Journal* article (15 October 1986) chronicles how the once formidable American free trade lobby is now in a shambles, and that free trade backers are expressing a rising doubt that the trade deficit can be addressed through conventional means. The weakening of the dollar against other major currencies is expected to moderate the deficit somewhat, as domestic goods become cheaper for foreigners, and foreign goods become more dear for Americans. But even massive adjustments in currency values are not likely to overcome the haemorrhaging.

It appears that the US and Japanese economies are on a collision course. Some experts have been so bold as to lay the burden upon the Japanese. Says Gary R. Saxonhouse, an economist at the University of Michigan, quoted in the 12 May 1985 issue of the *Seattle Times*: 'It is unfortunate but necessary that we must encourage Japan to have their economy look more like ours . . . but the legitimacy of the international economic system is at stake.' In testimony before two House Subcommittees looking into America's trade deficit, Saxonhouse and others urged the Japanese to save less, to consume more and to work fewer hours per week.

THE NEW WORLD ECONOMY

International trade expert Ray Waldmann points out that the world economy is disintegrating because it no longer fits the classical model. International trade doesn't rely upon market forces, but instead responds increasingly to the forces of intervention by nationalist governments. An estimated 25 to 30 per cent of all international trade is so controlled.[1]

Government disinvolvement in international trade has been the *sine qua non* of the conventional wisdom since the Great Depression. The Smoot–Hawley Tariff of 1930 is cited as a negative outcome of government protectionism. It was passed to stimulate domestic production and therefore employment, at the expense of foreign production and employment. But reciprocal tariffs by our trading partners led to a decline in the level of international trade, exacerbating the Depression era declines in domestic production, employment and living standards.

Congress abrogated the Smoot–Hawley Tariff with the passage of the Reciprocal Trade Act of 1934. It allows the President to negotiate to reduce tariffs up to 50 per cent, and to award 'most favoured nation status' to any trading partner, thereby allowing that partner to gain the best terms of trade that have previously been awarded to any other trading partner. Then, in 1947, twenty-three nations including the United States became signatories to the General Agreement on Tariffs and Trade (GATT). Basically, GATT is a forum for negotiating reductions in tariff barriers on a multilateral basis. Some 100 nations participated in GATT trade negotiations, known as the 'Tokyo Round', which were completed in 1979.

Although GATT has been successful in the reduction or elimination of tariffs, international trade has been impeded, particularly recently, by a variety of non-tariff barriers including import quotas, licensing requirements, arbitrary product quality standards, elaborate and unnecessary customs procedures, and so forth. GATT has become overloaded beyond the original intent of its founders. Some of these pressures have been caused by a recent explosion in international manufacturing in previously underdeveloped countries, made possible by the discovery and dissemination of new processes and technologies. The outcome has rendered the viable management of international trade by GATT increasingly untenable. Product counterfeiting, which has grown alarmingly in recent years, has further added to these pressures.

The contemporary goal of developing nations is to industrialize into higher value-added exports. Generally, countries do not seek to become merely exporters of raw materials. Also, as Waldmann points out, there has developed an increased interest by trading nations to exercise a high level of control over their economic destinies. This emphasis has led many nations to undertake massive investments in subsidized products, such as computers and supersonic aircraft, to name but two. Nationalistic-oriented investments have been undertaken in some cases even though the market for the output has not been readily apparent. The trend towards an increased presence for nation states in the endeavour of commerce is a direct challenge to the assumptions upon which the doctrine of free trade rests.

RICARDIAN FREE TRADE

David Ricardo is the principal behind free trade ideology. He reasoned that if two countries are isolated and self-sufficient, and if each has an opportunity-cost advantage in one of two goods produced, then each should specialize in the good in which it has the advantage, and rely upon international trade rather than domestic production to produce the other. Specialization and trade result in a more efficient allocation of world resources, a larger output of all traded goods, and therefore an increase in the material wealth of all participating countries.

International trade in Ricardo's model is a substitute for the international mobility of resources. Since it is reasoned that land is stationary, and surely that capital and labour are unlikely to be mobile in a nineteenth-century world view, production is also considered to be stationary. Only consumption is made mobile through trade. So the case for free trade is based upon some critical assumptions about resource immobility conveyed implicitly in a nineteenth-century world view.

Since Ricardian theory argues for free international trade, it also abhors any impediments to trade such as revenue or protective tariffs, import quotas, or other restrictive trade practices. These are portrayed as violations of the collective order necessary to sustain free international trade. Violations necessarily impede the development of living standards of participating countries. Like the Smoot–Hawley Tariff, they are alleged to invoke a tragedy of the commons. Whereas they may serve the advantage of isolated nations, if everyone practises them they engender a stagnation of economic progress. To the extent that protectionism fosters inefficient production, worldwide, then it also fosters a decline in the living standards of the world trading community.

RESTRICTIVE TRADE PRACTICES

In the contemporary international milieu, political expediency rather than the rationality of Ricardian-justified comparative advantage appears to rule the day. Protectionist measures such as trade embargos are frequently undertaken by national governments to keep out the unwanted products of foreign competitors. Arrangements often go beyond tariffs or quotas to take the form of health and safety inspections, or other restrictive practices. Bilateral agreements between trading nations may also limit trade with non-aligned or 'third party' nations.

The Japanese Government has been particularly successful at screening out foreign-produced goods through the application of subtle restrictive trade practices. But *The Wall Street Journal* of 1 November 1985 describes how the United States itself isn't the pure free-trader that many in Congress seem to think. Among the products and industries sheltered by US protectionism are sugar, books and periodicals, ceramic tiles, peanuts, rubber shoes, motorcycles, cars and light trucks. The Jones Act also bars foreign ships from carrying passengers or freight between US ports.

'Voluntary' import agreements restricting Japanese cars have been utilized in this decade. Other restrictive practices of the US Government are less well known. Indeed, significant trade barriers cover more than one quarter of all foreign manufactured goods marketed in the United States. For instance, foreign manufactured light trucks face a 25 per cent tariff at American ports of entry. This tariff prompted the creation of the Subaru 'Brat' which then escaped the tariff by putting bucket seats in the truck bed to qualify it as a car.

Over all, the pace of protectionism has increased dramatically in recent years. Since 1975, the percentage covered by protectionism has risen from 8 per cent to 21 per cent of all American imports. Although the United States may be less protectionist than Europe, and certainly less protectionist than Japan, the mounting level of protectionism has prompted Robert Z. Lawrence of the Brookings Institution to comment that Americans 'ought not to be necessarily as self-righteous as we are'.

Some commentators on international trade argue that even though its dimensions have changed dramatically, compensating actions by the US Government can stay the perilous times. Financier Felix Rohatyn, for instance, proposes temporary protection to our most threatened industries, conditional upon their commitments to become more competitive.[2] Defenders of free trade typically argue for bold and hopefully short-term measures to stem the tide of red ink in the nation's balance of trade accounts. Proposals include measures to control product counterfeiting, to re-endorse reciprocity, and to 'beef up' trade laws such as those which regulate product dumping or limit foreign predatory competition. The latter describes a practice in which foreign producers are accused of unjust pricing of raw materials.

Unfortunately, we shall ultimately acknowledge, with a floodtide of red ink before us, that the concept of free trade is outmoded and unworkable in today's world. There are various reasons for this. We shall deal with the most important one last.

DEATH OF FREE TRADE

If for no other reason, Ricardian free trade is unworkable in the latter decades of the twentieth century because the world is fundamentally different from the vision portrayed in Ricardo's free trade model. Labour and capital were essentially stationary until the middle of the twentieth century. This is true no longer in our technological world of communication and transportation.

Colonization is perhaps the first illustration of resource mobility. Finance, and occasionally capital and labour were exported, for example, by the British Commonwealth to enhance domestic wealth creation. In the twentieth century, guest worker policies, especially popular in the labour shortage economies of Western Europe during the 1960s, were strategies for overcoming labour immobility. These policies, which have since fallen from favour, represented a weakening, even though slight, in the immobility or resources assumption of the theoretical model.

But the big shift effecting the logic of the Ricardian model began in the 1970s with bold new trafficking in tangible capital and finance. The United States, which had faced the onslaught of low-cost Japanese-produced steel during the 1960s, now discovered that steel-making technology was being exported further afield to less developed countries. In the 1970s it was low-wage nations such as South Korea that challenged established steel markets not only in the United States, but in Japan as well. Entrepreneurs in the developing nations were discovering how to import new technologies from the industrialized West, undercut competition with low-cost labour, and then send the finished products into the markets of mature economies where it flourished because it was priced attractively.

The difficulties experienced by domestic manufacturing industries competing with low-cost imports became a national spectacle during the recession of 1981–2. The American steel industry is a particularly poignant example of this displacement. Even though the American labour force is the best educated in the world, and therefore highly productive, steel and other key industries have been ravaged by foreign operated technologies utilizing a cheap labour advantage.

Resource mobility is by no means limited to tangible capital. The free trade paradigm is being challenged, perhaps most provocatively, by the export of finance. By the 1970s sophisticated financial markets had developed in all parts of the industrial world, including Southeast Asia. Computerization makes it literally possible to 'shoot finance around the globe at the speed of light'. The opportunities for new forms of entrepreneurship based upon financial mobility are virtually unlimited.

American entrepreneurs and financiers teamed up with foreign counterparts during the 1970s to form formidable consortia. Production and fabrication facilities could be developed in the United States and then transported to low-wage nations and operated with low-cost labour. Of course, the output was then shipped back to the United States and to other mass markets to compete favourably with higher wage domestic goods.

For Americans, the new internationalism reveals itself as a two-edged sword. For Americans as consumers, it is a bonanza. Cheap and typically well-made goods produced with low-cost foreign labour in the 1980s represent an attractive reprieve from the inflationary 1970s. For instance, consider women's and girls' clothing which is produced amply in developing nations and marketed widely in the United States. It is one of the best bargains on merchants' shelves. Since 1967, the price index for women's and girls' clothing has increased by slightly over half of the increase in the price index for all consumer goods.

But for many Americans as producers, the new configuration in international trade has not served so well. Jobs in high-wage industries have been continuously lost to foreign competition. And much of that foreign competition has been initiated under the stewardship of American entrepreneurs and financiers who have gone overseas to do business. They have recognized the new mobilities of capital and finance, and have profited handsomely. But domestic workers in traditional manufacturing industries have not been so fortunate. Workers who lose their jobs in high-wage industries such as steel, wood products or extraction, typically are relocated, eventually, into lower wage service or retailing jobs. Fringe benefits in these industries are usually lower than in manufacturing, and often they are non-existent. These readjustments are likely to continue so long as cost advantages tempt manufacturers to flee outside the United States. And all the while Americans, as workers, are becoming poorer relative to a new class of nations reaping economic growth.

THE CRUCIAL REASON

Fleeing domestic industries, falling domestic wages, and the increased mobility of economic resources are only a partial explanation for the impending break-up of the world economy. The pre-eminent reason which builds upon all the others is that the second glitch of economic theory has destroyed the Ricardian logic that protectionism ultimately hurts everyone.

Passage of the Smoot–Hawley Tariff revealed a tragedy of the commons. When reciprocity made protectionism widespread among America's contemporary trading partners, everyone suffered. Because domestic exports fell, domestic output and employment was also lower. Unlike the 1930s, not everyone loses in the new regimen of restrictive international trade. Developing nations with cheap labour and access to sophisticated technology are reaping marvellous benefits. The economic fortunes of countries in the northern Pacific Rim are surely prospering. At the same time, the United States and other established industrial economies, to the extent that they remain non-protectionist, are losing jobs and income from the onslaught of low-cost imports.

Government-initiated protectionism by the developing nations is rewarding to those nations which practise it, so long as high-wage industrial trading partners do not reciprocate. For them, higher value added exports can be gained through the pursuit of policies which shelter infant industries, channel low-cost finance to key export industries, and otherwise generally follow the path of Japan. But even if these countries ultimately experience widespread reciprocity by the United States and other industrial nations, government intervention in trade will not become viewed as a curse, as it was following the Smoot–Hawley Tariff. The reason is that indicative economic planning, which has heretofore benefited developing nations in international trade, has become essential to the health of all nations in their domestic economies as well.

The second glitch of economic theory can only be corrected by the exogenous specification of the rate of profit. Otherwise, the blurring of the distinction between interest and profit, and therefore inadequate incentives to skill and industry, are likely to be revealed in a zero-growth outcome. Indicative economic planning has been a luxury to those who have pursued it. But it is a luxury no more. Since it has become revealed as essential to domestic prosperity, a fallacy of the commons no longer exists with regard to the intervention of governments in either domestic or foreign commerce. Countries are being forced to practise it at home, regardless of their desire to practise it abroad.

Free trade is doomed because it is illogical in the new economic order. It flies in the face of the requirement that national governments must intervene to produce favourable economic outcomes for their citizens. And it is only made more rapidly obsolete by the forces of international competition which drive contemporary economies towards its adoption.

JAPANESE CONQUEST

Japan's strategy has become legendary, as it has been repeated in one industrial conquest after another. Contemporary headlines chronicle how Asian computer firms have invaded the US market for personal computers. The 10 January 1986 issue of *The Wall Street Journal* points out that after five years of false starts, Asian manufacturers have quietly invaded the American personal computer market and seized at least 20 per cent of the $22 billion a year business. In many computer stores this past Christmas the fastest selling models were Japanese and Korean. The demand for these low-cost clones of popular American-developed technology like IBM's PC has been so strong that many dealers have been forced to ration their scarce supply of foreign machines. Beyond personal computers, Asian manufacturers now dominate certain markets for components such as monitors, disk drives and memory chips. Now Asian concerns are investing in high technology ventures that promise possible dominance in software and supercomputers.

This remarkable market penetration is contributing noticeably to the fast-growing US trade deficit which now approaches $50 billion yearly with Japan alone. The American Electronics Association estimates the 1985 electronics component of the deficit to be $8 billion. In 1983, the US boasted a $1.5 billion surplus in electronics. Some experts are predicting that what happened in cassette recorders, calculators, stereos, televisions and video cassette recorders is now happening in personal computers and related products. The Asians began by supplying parts like memory chips to US manufacturers. Then higher value added manufacturing led them to disk drives, and finally to fully assembled personal computers. Ultimately, their strength may be revealed in the dominance of supercomputers, minicomputers, and even mainframes.

The Japanese strategy is a finely honed subset of the Asian strategy. Sony Corporation's dominance of mini compact disc audio players, or mini-CDs, is an insightful case. Another *Wall Street Journal* article dated 28 February 1986 describes the slow entrance of Sony in the drive to develop laser technology that was initially pioneered by the

Dutch firm N.V. Phillips. Sony's triumph is a classic export triumph. It shows not only how the Japanese company succeeded, but also why some US competitors failed in the process. American firms such as RCA and Zenith invested hundreds of millions of dollars in disk research, only to abandon most of their projects. Now, Sony is expanding the technology into computer and military applications, and most US firms are out of the running.

Sony's success is described as a story of perseverance, luck, and aggressive marketing. When US companies became entrenched, they dropped out. Not so with the Japanese. Perhaps Japanese companies such as Sony are better prepared to face financial disappointment because they are less oriented to short-term profits. Because their organizations and financing are better secured against short-term fluctuations in profitability, the Japanese are better able to weather defeat and disappointment that would provoke reorganization of typical American ventures. This orientation to long-term 'pay outs' is a part of the culture which translates into individual corporate strategies. It is also supported by government initiatives that substantially favour successful long-run outcomes, in spite of the attractiveness of many shorter term outcomes that could otherwise prove fatal.

What may be the *coup de grâce* to the superiority of the American minicomputer industry was announced at an international electronics conference in March of 1986. Sony and North American Phillips have now developed a new category of consumer products based upon the mini compact disk concept. The new product will be available starting in 1987 for about $1000. The development appears to eclipse efforts to develop industry standards for computer memory stored peripherally on compact disks. Instead, a single five-inch disk can hold as much data as 1500 floppy disks, thereby allowing the user to interact directly with her data base, rather than peripherally.[3]

Among the interesting case studies, recently, is the shake-up of the American memory chip firm, Micron. In the fiscal year ending in August 1984, Micron realized $29 million in profit on $84 million in sales. But in 1985 the market for Micron's memory chips disintegrated in one of the steepest price collapses in electronics history. Haemorrhaging with losses, the Boise-based company fired half its workforce and shut down one of its two production lines. In mid-1985 Micron formally accused the Japanese semiconductor industry of illegally flooding the US with microchips sold at a loss. The charge was contained in a $300 million antitrust lawsuit against six Japanese electronics manufacturers. But a preliminary government ruling on

Micron's case, although supporting the basic charge that the Japanese microchip industry violated US trade law, found that violations weren't severe enough to explain the price gap between Micron and the Japanese competition.[4]

Many experts in the electronics and finance industries believe that Micron's decline is rooted in microeconomic factors which scattered tariff protection can't affect. These include the sheer size of Japanese firms, their access to low-cost finance, and their willingness and ability to wage long-term battles for market share at the expense of short-term profits. Again, expert opinion is that the semiconductor industry may be only the latest case of an American industry that is losing ground to Japan.

POLITICIZATION OF INTERNATIONAL TRADE

The old economic order that has existed in the free world since the Second World War is disintegrating. There exists no way to revive it. We have considered how government intervention in domestic economic decisions is necessary to domestic growth. Those economies which are benefiting from indicative economic planning cannot be dissuaded rationally from doing so, for it is a necessary correction to the operational framework of neoclassical economics.

Government involvement in both domestic and international economic issues is no longer a voluntary option, but a requirement of economic health. To embrace a broader role for government is inescapable. Attempts to rejoin the lost world of free trade can only exacerbate the depletion of time and resources. A new order is being born. Rather than existing upon principles of free trade, it will be based upon principles of economic nationalism and political expediency. Buy and sell will be only components of a much grander strategy. The use of trade will become a major component, perhaps the most significant component, of foreign policy. International alliances of the future will be cemented upon bilateral and multilateral trade agreements. Trade concessions will become integral to the negotiation of national security agreements. And shifting patterns of international commerce will inevitably signal shifting ideological allegiances.

11 Reaganomics

Ronald Reagan came to power with a mandate to purge the economy of the ills of Keynesianism. Since the Federal Reserve had already begun the task a full year ahead of the Republican landslide of 1980, momentum was well under way. Among the architects of the *laissez-faire* resurgence, or 'supply-siders', was Arthur Laffer who argued for a reduction in tax rates. According to the supply-siders, a cut in tax rates would stimulate output and income, and therefore generate a larger federal base from which tax revenues could be drawn. So even though rates might be cut, the end result would be an increase in total tax revenues.

Up to this point Reaganomics sounds like 'born again Keynesianism'. The supply-side rationale is similar to Keynesian arguments for the tax cut of 1964. But beyond the agreed upon attractiveness of a tax stimulus, the logic of the Keynesians and the supply-siders differs dramatically. For the former, which advocates a demand-driven stimulus to solve unemployment problems, the tax cut should go to the poor who are likely to consume a very high portion of it, and save only a small residue. The Keynesian national income multiplier increases in efficiency with increases in the marginal propensity to consume. Keynesian tax cut proposals have been directed more at the poor than at the rich. The latter have relatively low marginal propensities to consume.

But the supply-siders' tax cut proposal had as its recipient a very different target group. Since it was a supply driven formula for stimulating investment, its advocates reasoned that tax cuts should be directed away from the poor and towards the more well to do. It is the latter who are more likely to save and to invest. Their marginal propensity to consume is lower, and therefore their marginal propensity to save is higher.

The Economic Recovery Tax Act of 1981 (ERTA) was accompanied by stringent budget reduction provisions, included partly as an appeasement to conservatives who wanted to contain government spending. It was won at the cost of wrenching cuts in social welfare programmes. Because of this, detractors have called Reaganomics a 'trickle down' approach, meaning that it benefits the poor only indirectly, through the charity and the consumption of the rich. One popular view has portrayed ERTA not as an efficiency measure, but principally as a redistributional effort. Allegedly it recompensates the wealthy for their relative losses in the 1960s when Great Society social programmes were financed through somewhat stronger claims against the incomes of the well to do.[1]

Ronald Reagan received a second stunning electoral mandate in the presidential election of 1984. His economic platform was very similar to his platform of 1980, but with one particularly poignant exception. By 1984 the logic of ERTA had not been proven. With dramatically reduced federal revenues, deficits were reaching stratospheric highs. So Reagan's revised economic 'game plan' adopted a justification for deficit spending, in spite of the reality that he had spent a lifetime opposing it.

According to Reagan and his running mate George Bush, Americans by 1984 had once again regained optimism and faith. Gigantic increases in the federal debt were treated as a temporary but necessary artifact on the road back to prosperity. Again the candidates campaigned and won on the platform that national despair and pessimism had been spawned by years of Democratic overspending and overtaxation. Productivity, industrial production and real wages were down when they took office in 1981, they said. The only things that had been going up during the Carter years were taxes and the size of government. Since inflation and taxes reduce the reward for hard work, thrift and entrepreneurial risktaking, the candidates asserted that a bold new path had been proclaimed by the Reagan economic plan. It just needed time to work, and the faith of American voters, they said. 'Aren't you better off now,' the candidates queried, 'than you were four years ago?' The electorate responded with a resounding yes.

ARE WE BETTER OFF?

At the time of writing, the second quarter of 1986, it is instructive to ask a variation on the Reagan–Bush theme: Are Americans better off as the result of economic policies of the Reagan administration? For an initial long-range perspective, consider that GNP grew from a Depression low of $222 billion in 1933 (measured in 1972 dollars) to $1058 billion, thirty-five years later in 1968. During that same period the population grew from 126 million to 201 million people. On a per capita basis, the American economy experienced a real, threefold improvement in the standard of living. American citizens were able

Table 11.1 Gross national product in 1982 dollars (billions)

Year	Gross national product	Per cent change from preceding period
1973	2744.1	5.2
1974	2729.3	−.5
1975	2695.0	−1.3
1976	2826.7	4.9
1977	2958.6	4.7
1978	3115.2	5.3
1979	3192.4	2.5
1980	3187.1	−.2
1981	3248.8	1.9
1982	3166.0	−2.5
1983	3279.1	3.6
1984	3489.9	6.4
1985	3585.2	2.7
1986ᴾ	3676.5	2.5

ᴾ preliminary

to consume three times as large a quantity of goods and services in 1968 as comparable citizens consumed in 1933.

Productivity is the main contributor to economic growth, and therefore to improvement in the living standard. Factor productivity grew at a rate of 3.1 per cent over the twenty-year period between 1948 and 1968. After 1968, however, productivity improvement dropped off markedly. Between 1968 and 1979, it grew at a compound rate of 1.4 per cent. And between 1979 and 1984, its rate of growth averaged 1.6 per cent. Indeed, Reaganomics has had no significant impact upon productivity improvement (Tables 11.1–11.2).

In many countries the post-Vietnam War productivity declines have been even greater than in the United States. Among the factors widely attributed to the slide are a younger and less experienced workforce, government regulation, higher energy prices (prior to 1986), and reduced research and development. Economist Lester Thurow describes these multiple sources as 'death by a thousand cuts'. As Barry Bosworth (1984) points out, each of many factors implicit in productivity decline contributes only a few tenths of a per cent annually. The likelihood is that several contributors to productivity soured simultaneously and coincidentally. According to Bosworth, the major conclusion that emerges from productivity studies in recent years 'is that the productivity slowdown is, in large part, a mystery'.

Table 11.2 Productivity and earnings, 1977 = 100

Year	Index of hourly earnings adjusted for inflation	Average gross weekly non-farm earnings	Non-farm output per hr.
1965	89.0	183.21	83.4
1966	90.3	184.37	85.2
1967	92.2	184.83	87.1
1968	94.0	187.68	89.4
1969	95.0	189.44	89.0
1970	95.7	186.94	89.3
1971	98.3	190.58	91.9
1972	101.2	198.41	94.7
1973	101.1	198.35	96.4
1974	98.3	190.12	94.3
1975	97.6	184.16	96.0
1976	99.0	186.85	98.5
1977	100.0	189.00	100.0
1978	100.5	189.31	100.8
1979	97.4	183.41	99.3
1980	93.5	172.74	98.8
1981	92.6	170.13	99.8
1982	93.4	168.09	99.2
1983	94.9	171.26	102.4
1984	94.6	172.78	104.3
1985	94.1	170.42	104.8
1986*	94.9	171.07	N

* preliminary
N not given

Economist Lawrence H. Summers (1984) echoes this same senti-
ment: 'The simple fact is that we as a profession do not have any clear
idea of how to reverse the productivity slowdown, which dramatically
reduced worldwide prosperity'. Of course, it is the assertion of this
book that a substantial part of the productivity decline results from
hoarding, in which productively held assets are transferred to non-
productive use.

Declining productivity leads to a declining standard of living. Real
hourly compensation – a good indicator of the living standard – has
fallen from a compound growth rate of just over 3 per cent in the
twenty-year period ending in 1967, to 2.0 per cent for the period
between 1968 and 1973, to 0.3 per cent in the eleven-year period
between 1974 and 1985.

THE EXPERTS DISAGREE

In the first half of 1986 there continues to be mixed signals about the performance of the American economy. The pessimists and the optimists tell very different stories. From the optimist's point of view, the economic recovery since 1982 has been among the most buoyant ever. Inflation has been tamed to the 3 to 4 per cent level, from double-digit levels prevailing earlier. Interest rates have moderated. Mortgage interest rates entered back into the single digit realm for the first time since 1979. Unemployment remains somewhat high, but politically acceptable. And business economists generally consider consumer confidence to be strong, investment forecasts to be favourable, and the prognosis for a lingering recovery to be healthy. The stock market has entered previously uncharted territory. Dramatic declines in the price of crude oil in the first half of 1986 further accentuated the rosy outlook.

The pessimists, on the other hand, point to longer term indicators of economic malaise including poor productivity and poor earnings performance. They focus upon the national deficit, the trade imbalance, and an increasingly unequal distribution of income. Long-term data vaunted by the pessimists are sobering indeed. They also point to instability in the indicators of short-term economic performance, which makes the optimistic view somewhat less sanguine. As Laurie McGinley of *The Wall Street Journal* on 12 August 1985 pointed out, when consumer confidence is high retail sales should be good. However, recent evidence does not confirm this, nor does contemporary experience verify the expectation that when the stock market is high the economy should be growing. At the historical apex of the stock market growth seems to be stalled.

'Mixed signals and unknown variables' are derided as unsettling factors. In fact, the gap between the most optimistic and the most pessimistic of business forecasts is unusually wide and growing wider. According to John Langum, president of Business Economics Inc. of Chicago, 'The economy is like a car skidding on ice. It is difficult to know where it will end up.' Analysts frequently cite changes in inventory practices and demographics, the political influence of the Federal Reserve, and the growing and fundamentally changing role of the world economy, as some of the reasons for the consternation. Indeed, it seems that economic science has lost some of its ability to explain and to predict. And the denizens of this apparent failing of

Table 11.3   Changes in the consumer price index, 1967 = 100

Year	All items	Rate of change
1956	81.4	1.5
1957	84.3	3.6
1958	86.6	2.7
1959	87.3	.8
1960	88.7	1.6
1961	89.6	1.0
1962	90.6	1.1
1963	91.7	1.2
1964	92.9	1.3
1965	94.5	1.7
1966	97.2	2.9
1967	100.0	2.9
1968	104.2	4.2
1969	109.8	5.4
1970	116.3	5.9
1971	121.3	4.3
1972	125.3	3.3
1973	133.1	6.2
1974	147.7	11.0
1975	161.2	9.1
1976	170.5	5.8
1977	181.5	6.5
1978	195.4	7.7
1979	217.4	11.3
1980	246.8	13.5
1981	272.4	10.4
1982	289.1	6.1
1983	298.4	3.2
1984	311.3	4.3
1985	322.2	3.6
1986	328.4	1.9

economic science have come to be regarded by many American citizens with disenchantment, if not scorn.

FEDERAL DEFICITS

The disappointing progress of the American economy prior to Ronald Reagan's election in 1980 is widely acknowledged. Growth had been sluggish, particularly since 1973, and Federal deficits mounted

Table 11.4 Deficit of the federal government, cumulative debt and
interest cost of debt service (billions of dollars)

Year	Annual deficit (or surplus)	Cumulative debt	Interest cost*
1940	2.9	50.7	
1945	47.6	260.1	
1950	3.1	256.9	
1955	3.0	274.4	
1960	.3	290.9	
1965	1.4	323.2	
1970	2.8	382.6	
1971	23.0	409.5	
1972	23.4	437.3	
1973	14.9	468.4	
1974	6.1	486.2	
1975	53.2	544.1	
1976	73.7	631.9	
1977	53.6	709.1	
1978	59.2	780.4	35.4
1979	40.2	833.8	42.6
1980	73.8	914.3	52.5
1981	78.9	1003.9	68.7
1982	127.9	1147.0	84.9
1983	207.8	1381.9	89.7
1984	185.3	1576.7	111.0
1985	212.3	1827.2	129.4
1986	220.7	2132.9	136.0

* Not given prior to 1978

as monuments to the illogic of contemporary Keynesian practices. In
1981, within the first year of the Reagan presidency, the cumulative
national debt surpassed the 1 trillion dollar mark. According to the
president, the occasion 'stood as a monument' to the defunct Keynesian
policies of his Democratic predecessor. And those policies, according
to Reagan, were reversed with the signing of ERTA in 1981.

Table 11.4 chronicles the progress of federal deficit spending since
1940. It is quite evident that Ronald Reagan did not repudiate
Keynesian economics by his initiatives to control deficit spending.
Instead, the red ink exploded under his leadership. By 1985, in the
fifth year of the Reagan presidency, the cumulative federal debt
surpassed the 2 trillion dollar mark. But by then the event could not
be conveniently labelled as an artifact of the Carter administration. It
was Reagan's own doing.

Interest costs of servicing the public debt have grown particularly oppressive. Keynesians in the 1950s and 1960s often justified 'functional finance' as benign, because it was a debt that the American public owes to itself. But so often in public policy the arcane wisdom of the pedants is eventually revealed to be imprudent. Apart from the reality that foreigners own an increasing portion of the national debt, the real issue of the size of national debt is one of opportunity cost. Given a bounded set of federal revenues, the opportunity cost of servicing America's debt is the value of programmes that could have been implemented, instead, if the debt had not been incurred. And this cost extends into perpetuity, to the next generation, and to each subsequent generation.

In 1985, the interest cost of servicing the federal debt was nearly 2.5 times as great as in 1980: the year of Mr Reagan's election. To provide some standard of comparison, the amount spent on interest in 1985 was about equal to the cost of all income security programmes, excluding social security. Or, it was about two-thirds the size of the social security programme, or about one half of all expenditures for national defence.

Clearly, the optimistic revenue projections by the tax cut's sponsors failed to materialize and a deficit explosion resulted. According to estimates by the Office of Management and Budget (OMB) made for FY 1984, ERTA cost about $125 billion in tax revenues forgone in each of the five years following its passage. Since deficits have been running in the $200 billion range,[2] we conclude that at least one half of the size of current deficits is attributable to ERTA. Alternately stated, federal deficits would be less than half their current size if the tax cut had not been passed. Congress chose not to deal with the deficit issue in the context of the tax reform bill of 1986, choosing instead to make revisions to the Internal Revenue code 'revenue neutral'.

INVESTMENT

Unquestionably ERTA has been costly in revenue forgone. But what have American citizens received in exchange for the gargantuan deficits created in its wake? The supply-side defence has been that a reduction in tax rates favouring the well to do would ultimately be revealed in an increase in tax revenue. This would occur as individuals and businesses converted their new found saving into new investment. Presumably investment would embody the most advanced technology, fostering productivity improvement and economic growth.

However, since productivity and growth have not materialized as promised, it may be instructive to look at the intermediate effect of the tax cut upon investment. The *Economic Review* of the Federal Reserve Bank of Kansas City points out that investment spending has boomed since the beginning of the current economic expansion. But not all types of investment have shared equally in the recovery. Office equipment including computers, and cars purchased by businesses, accounted for 93 per cent of the rise in business spending between 1979 and 1984. But other sectors of equipment spending, including industrial, metal working and construction machinery, engines and turbines, and tractors, grew at a much slower rate than growth in total business equipment. Also, most recent investment studies contradict the view that ERTA was the primary cause of the investment boom.[3]

Fixed investment includes plant, equipment and residential construction. Note in Table 11.5 that in the six-year period from 1981 through 1985, fixed investment averaged $564 billion per year. This compares with an average of $489 billion in each of the six years preceding the passage of ERTA. So, while fixed investment has been buoyant in the recovery, its performance has not been impressive in view of the cost of obtaining it. Roughly speaking, an average improvement of $75 billion in net investment has been won at the cost of almost double that amount in annual tax revenue forgone.

It is true that fixed investment has increased in each year following ERTA's passage. Inflation accounts for a portion of this increase. In 1985, fixed investment was about 25 per cent higher than its 1980 level. If the rate of increase continued indefinitely, at some point it would grow to the magnitude of the annual cost of ERTA. But only then would lost revenue because of ERTA be equal to fixed investment. In other words, at that point all the yearly improvement in fixed investment would have been paid for by revenue forgone because of ERTA. The 'best case' scenario, then, is one of government paying dollar-for-dollar for investment increases in the private sector. The 'worst case' scenario is one of government recouping only a fraction of the revenue given away by ERTA. In either case the cost of ERTA, if it is justified by increases in fixed investment, is enormous.

Supply-siders have argued that the durability of the recovery may eventually vindicate ERTA on efficiency grounds. But our calculations

Table 11.5   Fixed investment plant, equipment and residential
construction (billions of 1982 dollars)

Year	Total
1970	373.3
1971	399.7
1972	443.7
1973	480.8
1974	448.0
1975	396.1
1976	431.4
1977	492.2
1978	540.2
1979	560.2
1980	516.2
1981	521.7
1982	471.8
1983	510.4
1984	592.8
1985	638.6
1986*	648.9

* preliminary

show that the length of the recovery would need to be very long
indeed. Surely it would need to extend to the end of the decade
(1982–9) or beyond for even the most modest supply-side claims to be
vindicated – and such a durable recovery is unlikely. As economist
Irwin L. Kellner points out, only once in the past 130 years has the
economy grown for such an extended and uninterrupted interval.
That was the 106-month expansion that ended in the final quarter of
1969. Vietnam, of course, was ongoing during the latter years of this
expansion. In fact, the average post-war peacetime expansion has
lasted only thirty-four months, or eleven quarters.[4]

It appears that supply-side economics has been a costly ruse if it is
justified on the basis of anything other than a preference for income
redistribution. But, if the tax cut didn't stimulate investment, then
what, if anything (besides consumption), did it stimulate? What
became of the extra saving that was supposed to appear as investment?

Table 11.6 Saving behaviour (billions of dollars)

Year	Interest paid by government to foreigners	Net foreign investment	Personal saving as per cent of disposable personal income
1970	1.0	4.8	8.1
1971	1.8	1.3	8.5
1972	2.7	−2.9	7.3
1973	3.8	8.8	9.4
1974	4.3	5.4	9.3
1975	4.5	21.6	9.2
1976	4.5	9.0	7.6
1977	5.5	−8.7	6.6
1978	8.7	−10.1	7.1
1979	11.1	2.6	6.8
1980	12.6	13.0	7.1
1981	16.9	10.6	7.5
1982	18.3	−1.0	6.8
1983	17.8	−33.5	5.4
1984	19.8	−90.7	6.3
1985	21.3	−115.2	5.1
1986*	23.0	−143.7	3.9

* preliminary

INTEREST-BEARING ASSETS

It is likely that much of the saving that was initially generated by the tax cut went to some use other than fixed investment. Indeed, saving behaviour has been worrisome, recently, as Table 11.6 shows. For instance, the personal saving rate of 4.6 per cent in 1985, in which personal income was about $2.8 trillion, generated less total saving ($130 billion) than the amount of federal government dissaving ($212 billion). The dramatic difference between personal saving and federal dissaving was made up principally by an inflow of net foreign investment of $111 billion (negative). Net foreign investment by foreigners in the United States occurs when foreigners are attracted by high interest rates, or when foreign dollars are placed in American capital holdings. An example is the dramatic increase in ownership of American capital by Japanese interests.

The significance of the foreign ownership of American assets is profound. Between the First World War and 1985, the United States was a net creditor nation. Foreigners owed Americans more than Americans owed foreigners. This reversed in 1985, making America a net debtor nation and reflects the reality that foreigners hold increasing claims against American assets, including capital. This means that an increasing share of the non-labour component of personal income is accruing to foreigners. Not only is the ownership pattern of American assets changing, but the flow of income benefits to ownership is changing as well.

A declining rate of saving means that Americans are consuming more now, and by investing less, future consumption will be less than would result otherwise. This does not necessarily mean that total saving is declining, but rather that the percentage of personal income flowing into saving is declining. So we conclude that the post-ERTA rate of saving to fuel investment is smaller than expected. But at the same time we are also led to ask where much of saving has been placed, if it has not appeared in fixed investment as the supply-siders promised.

Table 11.7 may offer some clues. To interpret it effectively, we must begin with the inflationary 1970s. To protect their holdings, or to gain from speculation, many wealth-holders made placements in inelastically supplied assets such as real estate. Shortly after the election of Ronald Reagan in 1980, the writer lunched with one of the members of Reagan's so-called 'kitchen cabinet'. His view was that the economy had been badly managed by the Democrats, and that there existed perhaps one last chance to straighten it out. Since many transactors had come to hold their wealth in real estate and other inelastically supplied assets, he argued that a reduction of inflation and a substantial tax incentive would stimulate the entrepreneurial spirit. Wealth would be coaxed out of hiding in non-productive placements, and it would be reinvested in fixed capital and other equities instead.

On the contrary, it appears that savvy transactors did something quite different with their wealth holdings in the early 1980s. Largely as a response to the tight money policy implemented by the Federal Reserve beginning in 1979, interest rates soared. The action did serve to 'wring' inflation out of the economy. But higher interest rates also triggered extensive portfolio-shifting. Rather than moving from real estate directly to fixed investment, however, many savvy transactors moved from holding inelastically supplied goods, to holding interest-bearing finance instead.

Table 11.7 Some interest-bearing components of money stock and measures of liquid assets (billions of dollars)

Year	Demand deposits	Other checkable deposits	Overnight RPs	General purpose money market mutual funds	Money market deposit accounts
1970	166.3	.1	1.3	.0	.0
1971	176.9	.2	2.3	.0	.0
1972	193.7	.2	2.8	.0	.0
1973	202.4	.3	5.3	.1	.0
1974	207.4	.4	5.6	1.7	.0
1975	214.1	.9	5.8	2.7	.0
1976	224.3	2.7	10.6	2.4	.0
1977	239.4	4.2	14.7	2.4	.0
1978	253.4	8.5	20.3	6.4	.0
1979	261.3	17.4	21.2	33.4	.0
1980	265.3	28.0	28.3	61.6	.0
1981	234.6	78.0	35.9	150.6	.0
1982	237.9	103.4	38.8	185.2	43.2
1983	242.7	131.3	53.8	138.2	379.2
1984	248.4	146.3	56.3	167.5	417.0
1985	271.5	178.6	70.3	176.5	512.0
1986*	307.8	232.7	75.7	207.2	570.7

* preliminary

THE NORTHWEST

One would expect the data to reveal that interest and other non-wage components of personal income are up dramatically. Such is the case. Table 11.8 reveals that income earned as personal interest more than doubled between 1979 and 1985. For the same period wage and salary income increased only about 60 per cent. Income data for the state of Washington, in which the writer resides, are particularly interesting in this regard. Washington has historically been an industrial state with a healthy economy and increasing ties with Asian international trade. A study by the Washington State Legislature, House Ways and Means Committee (1985), reveals that the non-wage component of personal income remained stable until about 1979. In the 1960s it averaged about 10 per cent of personal income. Things changed after 1978. But by 1985 it had risen to over 21 per cent of total personal income, and it is projected to reach 23 per cent

Public Policy

Table 11.8 Components of income (billions of dollars)

Year	Wage and salary	Rental income of persons	Personal dividend income	Personal interest income
1970	551.5	18.2	22.2	69.3
1971	583.9	18.6	22.6	74.7
1972	638.7	17.9	24.1	80.8
1973	708.7	18.0	26.6	93.3
1974	772.6	16.1	28.9	111.9
1975	814.6	13.5	28.7	122.5
1976	899.5	11.9	33.8	134.1
1977	993.9	8.2	38.2	155.4
1978	1119.3	9.3	43.0	182.5
1979	1252.1	5.6	48.1	221.5
1980	1372.0	6.6	52.9	271.9
1981	1510.3	13.3	61.3	335.4
1982	1586.1	13.6	63.9	369.7
1983	1676.6	13.2	68.7	393.1
1984	1836.8	8.3	74.7	446.9
1985	1966.1	7.6	76.4	476.2
1986*	2073.8	15.6	81.2	475.4

* preliminary

by 1987. The non-wage component includes interest, dividends and rent. It excludes income from pensions and rent earned by people not primarily engaged in real estate.

The same report shows that real per capita wages and salaries in the state have declined by over 10 per cent since 1978. A particular problem with the restructuring of the Washington economy, portrayed by these numbers, is that jobs in the growing sectors – such as retailing and services – pay substantially less than jobs in the declining sectors – including manufacturing, extraction, and lumber and wood products. A related study determined that the average wage per hour in Washington's eight fastest growing industries was $7.00, compared to $11.50 per hour in the eight major declining industries. While concluding that income distribution is becoming more unequal and that poverty is on the increase, the Washington State report adds that low wages appears to be replacing unemployment as the state's major economic problem.

This conclusion is supported by national data on productivity and earnings (Table 11.9). Real employee hourly compensation in 1985 was at the same level as first attained nine years earlier in 1976.

Table 11.9   Output and real compensation per hour, 1977 = 100

Year	Output per hour business sector	Real compensation* business sector
1968	87.6	87.6
1969	87.7	89.0
1970	88.3	90.1
1971	91.2	92.0
1972	94.1	94.9
1973	15.9	96.7
1974	13.9	95.4
1975	15.7	95.9
1976	98.3	98.7
1977	100.0	100.0
1978	100.8	100.8
1979	99.6	99.4
1980	99.3	96.7
1981	100.7	95.7
1982	100.3	97.3
1983	103.0	98.2
1984	105.3	98.1
1985	106.4	98.8

* Hourly compensation divided by the Consumer Price Index for all urban consumers

Another data set, average hourly non-farm earnings in 1985, adjusted for inflation, were at a level first attained in 1968. Depending upon the data chosen, this means that the average worker has gone between one and two decades without an improvement in purchasing power; a phenomenon that is rapidly becoming unprecedented in this century!

DISTRIBUTION

National data on the distribution of income indicate an increasingly unequal distribution of wealth throughout the United States. An Urban Institute study points out that between 1980 and 1984, the incomes of the poorest one-fifth of the national population declined by 7.6 per cent and the incomes of the richest fifth rose by 8.7 per cent.[5] Another recent study by Steve Rose (1985) of the Washington State Senate Ways and Means Committee indicates that the middle class in the US is shrinking. The middle class dropped from 52.3 per

Table 11.10   Income and poverty status

Year	Median income in 1984 dollars		Persons below, poverty level-millions			
	All families	Black only	All persons	Rate	Black	Rate
1970	26 394	16 796	25.4	12.6	7.5	33.5
1971	26 378	16 517	25.6	12.5	7.4	32.5
1972	27 599	17 042	24.5	11.9	7.7	33.3
1973	28 167	16 990	23.0	11.1	7.4	31.4
1974	27 175	16 863	23.4	11.2	7.2	30.3
1975	26 476	16 943	25.9	12.3	7.5	31.3
1976	27 293	16 863	25.0	11.8	7.6	31.1
1977	27 440	16 391	24.7	11.6	7.7	31.3
1978	28 085	17 321	24.5	11.4	7.6	30.6
1979	28 029	16 562	26.1	11.7	8.1	31.0
1980	26 500	15 976	29.3	13.0	8.6	32.5
1981	25 569	15 151	31.8	14.0	9.2	34.2
1982	25 216	14 633	34.4	15.0	9.7	35.6
1983	25 724	15 181	35.3	15.2	9.9	35.7
1984	26 433	15 432	33.7	14.4	9.5	33.8

cent to 44.3 per cent of the population between 1978 and 1985. This eight percentage point decline was offset by an increase of 5.2 percentage points in the bottom group and 2.8 percentage points in the top group. Thus, two-thirds of those exiting the middle class fell into a lower status. Rose's study indicates that half the decline in the middle class was due to a declining proportion of the population of husband–wife couples with both spouses present in the home.

The recent income and poverty status of American individuals is particularly illuminating (Table 11.10). The median income for American families in constant 1984 dollars was approximately the same fourteen years earlier, in 1970. But for black families, median income declined by 9 per cent over the same period. Poverty figures are even more devastating than the levelling, or decline of median family income. Between 1979 and 1984 the number of American families living below the poverty line increased by one-third. For black families, the incidence of poverty increased 24 per cent.

The distribution of America's wealth is substantially less egalitarian than the distribution of income. In 1986 the Democratic staff of the Joint Economic Committee of Congress released a study showing that the wealthiest 10 per cent of the households control 72 per cent of America's privately held net worth.[6] However, the study was challenged because of its limited sample of wealthy respondents, and on other methodological grounds. While the definitive study has yet to be reported, it does appear that an approximate 70–30 distribution of American wealth is not untenable. That is, the wealthiest 10 per cent of American households may control 70 per cent of the net worth, with the remaining 90 per cent of households controlling the balance of 30 per cent.

DECLINING AMERICA

In an in-depth look at poverty in the 1980s, Knight-Ridder Newspapers reported on interviews with poor people, public aid workers, government officials and academic experts around the country. Among the reported findings, there has been a sharp increase in the number of married couples who are poor, a group that historically has had a low poverty rate. Young people starting out on their own have been particularly hard hit. Among persons under 25 with their own households, 33 per cent lived in poverty in 1984, up from 20 per cent in 1979.[7]

Single-parent families continue to experience a disproportionate amount of poverty. Among families headed by women with school-age children, the poverty rate has increased from 36 per cent to 46 per cent since 1979. Alarmingly, the most rapid increase in poverty is being borne by children under 6 years of age. Overall, the number of children in poverty increased by an astounding 63 per cent between 1979 and 1984. One out of every five young children was living in poverty in 1984!

Related studies show that child abuse is dramatically on the rise, and that most children are victimized by their own family members who are increasingly frustrated by social and economic problems. The Child Welfare League of America reports that child abuse and neglect rose 16 per cent between 1983 and 1984. Even so, there exists no coordinated national effort to help suffering children or to monitor effectively these shameful trends nationwide.

THE AMERICAN DREAM

The American dream is in intensive care. It is the vision of intergenerational mobility: of living better than one's parents were able to live. As we are growing up we make subtle comparisons and these continue as we move throughout our lives. The middle-class dream has come to mean more material goods including a single-family home, one or two cars (including a new one), a washer and dryer, a dishwasher, colour TV, microwave and video recorder, and prospects for educating one's children and for a bountiful retirement. This dream is slipping beyond the typical American family's grasp.

Our society, as Lester Thurow describes it, has become a zero sum society. Not all Americans are becoming worse off. Some are, while others are simultaneously becoming better off. In a zero sum society, the only way that one can have more, is for someone else to have less. In responding to this static situation Americans have become more competitive. The drive to 'get yours' has become more intense. And ultimately, what has been called the 'yuppy (young urban professional) mentality' – which economist Thorsten Veblen called 'conspicuous consumption' – becomes rampant. As materialism and self-interest become more common, the well-being of those who are unable or ill-prepared to compete in market society is neglected.

Neglect seems to be the hallmark of the eighties. The American people, somehow, have become hardened to the problems of others, in a way that is historically uncharacteristic of Americans. Neglect of street people, of children living in poverty, of a growing underclass of Americans. Getting ahead is no longer assured, as it was for the parents or grandparents of maturing Americans. Now, economic success is too often associated with luck or high risk. Becoming a rock star or professional athlete, or winning a lottery or a law suit, may be the tatters of the fallen dream to which so many Americans cling.

Frank S. Levy and Richard C. Michel (1985) of the Urban Institute point out that while the overall distribution of income in the United States has not changed much during the last thirty five years, there have been substantial movements within it. In 1984, the middle quintile of families received exactly the same percentage of cash income as the middle quintile received in 1947, which is 17.0 per cent. The bifurcation of the middle class is largely an age-related phenomenon. What is concealed by the aggregate numbers is that some have been becoming better off, while others have been getting worse off. Those who are becoming better off tend to have reached 35 years of age prior to 1973. Younger cohorts are much more likely to experience decline in their economic fortunes, in comparison with comparable cohorts a decade or two ago.

The issue, according to the Urban Institute, is not so much a growing inequality of current income, but a growing inequality of prospects. The American dream of having more, or even as much as the preceding generation has faded. Those who already have it are likely to retain it, but those who haven't must ultimately recognize that their prospects have dimmed. To many families the resolution of this decline in expectations has meant trading off the opportunity to start families and to raise children. These are exchanged for more current consumption including houses, cars and retirement packages.

With the cost of necessities increasing, other items must give way. For instance, the average worker in the 1950s committed about 14 per cent of gross pay to housing. During the mid-1980s, a 30-year-old male who purchases a similar home must devote about 44 per cent of gross pay for that purpose . A young family in 1981 spent 14 per cent less on furniture, 30 per cent less on clothes, 15 per cent less on personal care and 38 per cent less on charitable contributions than a similar young family in 1973.

Saving is the final item to be relinquished. In 1981, young families saved less than 1 per cent of after-tax income, compared with 4 per cent for similar families in 1973. Almost 1 million more young families in 1984 had no savings whatever to fall back on in the event of an emergency. Of course, the less a family is able to save, the longer it must postpone its entrance into the housing market. And the greater its short-term debt, the less likely is its ability to qualify for a mortgage loan. For the nation as a whole, deficits and debt are ways in which Americans can temporarily live beyond their means. But in so doing, saving and investment which could lead to improved prospects are stymied. As the debt burden grows, the economic prospects for younger generations, even generations yet unborn, is diminished.[8]

DISTRIBUTIONAL GAMES

Zero sum society is more balkanized, and therefore it is likely to be more legalistic. If the prospect that almost everyone will become better off in the course of time does not exist, then competitive forces may intensify pressures to fight for and to win 'spoils' that might otherwise be ignored. Robert J. Samuelson points out that the United States now has more lawyers (675 000 of them) per capita

than any other major nation. Since the Second World War their
numbers have grown at a rate that is double the rate of population
growth. A rising tide of lawsuits is not the only reason for more
lawyers. More government regulation, complicated tax rules and
expanded international business have all contributed. But the growth
of lawsuits is the biggest factor in the burgeoning of the profession.[9]
Among the side-effects, says Samuelson, is the danger of becoming
a precautionary society. Unintended side-effects are already visible.
He points out that the threat of suits has driven some drug companies
from manufacturing vaccines; some consulting engineers refuse to
work on hazardous sites for fear of being sued; and companies are
losing outside directors for lack of liability coverage.

Newsweek's Jane Bryant Quinn, in the 30 December 1985 issue,
argues that our society, in part, has become a vast spoils system. She
says:

> Enormous amounts of time and energy are spent not in creating
> new wealth but in wrestling over the existing wealth. Adam Smith's
> idea was that societies prosper when everyone tries to get ahead,
> because profit-maximizing producers generate new wealth. But
> wealthy, complex societies injure Smith's hand. You can advance
> just as easily by grabbing someone else's wealth.

To the victor of legal contests, including corporate mergers, take-
overs and damage suits, go the spoils. People playing distributional
games by legally challenging the wealth of others, occupy some of
society's best minds, and at enormous social cost. No society, as
Ms Quinn points out, has a limitless talent for inventiveness. We
cannot expect society's wealth to expand if our precious resources are
occupied with the competitive activities of a zero sum society.

A FIRE SALE

As America continues its slide towards becoming a poorer nation,
unique proposals abound for settling short-term problems. The concept of 'privatization' of the assets of the federal government to
reduce the deficit is becoming popular. But it is rather analogous to a
rescue strategy for saving the *Titanic* that involves the mere rearrangement of the deck chairs. The rationale for privatization is
largely doctrinaire. It is a product of conservative, even libertarian

thinking that favours the minimization of both government size and government role.

According to economic adviser Thomas Moore, who heads the president's privatization task force, 'We're looking at everything that can be privatized in one way or another. Sold off or contracted out. Anything that can get the governmental job done more cheaply and efficiently.'[10] Proposals for privatization include the sale of Conrail, the Naval Petroleum Reserves, electrical power-generating and distributing networks such as the Bonneville Power Administration, Washington National and Dulles airports, the Federal Housing Administration, and the US Postal Service.

Amidst such radical proposals it is interesting, perhaps frightening, to consider the public mood in the first quarter of 1986. After five years of leadership by Ronald Reagan, the enormity of the problem is before us. It is not entirely the doing of Ronald Reagan and the conservatives, nor can it be laid entirely at the feet of his predecessors, the liberal Keynesians. But neither solution seems to hold much promise for the future. In the vacuum of ideas, American policy is likely to vacillate back and forth between inflationary policies on the one hand, and monetary stringency on the other.

But the most disconcerting reality is the passivity of the American public. We seem to ignore, to endure, and to live on the hope that the American dream will be refurbished by someone in authority, sometime soon. But the reality is that it will not, and that no one is in charge – that no one has the answers – is indeed sobering. When will Americans ultimately acknowledge that their frame of reference, their lives, are fundamentally and irrevocably different from the economic lives of the generation before?

DEFERRING THE PAIN

Over the past decade Americans have done a marvellous job of denying reality. Unfortunately, the longer America postpones the inevitable accounting, the weaker the economic system will be, and the less resilient will be its capacity for self-renewal. Among the many ways that the American public has forestalled recognition of the inevitable is in the deferral of loan losses. About 465 savings and loans ended 1985 by operating in insolvency. The estimated cost of liquidating these thrifts – in public funds – is $14 billion. Because they are ultimately insured by the Federal Saving and Loan Insurance

Corporation (FSLIC), they can continue to operate while the red ink continues to mount. Ultimately, it is American taxpayers who are liable for making good on the losses. FSLIC is not alone in its perils. The top ten US banks continue to carry at full value about $55 billion in loans to five major Latin American nations and to the Philippines. The true worth of the loans, according to many analysts, could be 20 to 50 per cent of their face value. Another $70 billion of debt is in trouble in the Farm Credit System. Recent legislation shifts much of this bad debt to a separate corporation that may ultimately require a substantial federal bail-out. The farm debt problem is exacerbated by the Agriculture Department's Farmers Home Administration which is carrying billions of dollars of bad loans on its books. Further, the steep decline in world oil prices in the first half of 1986 is likely to trigger a new round of energy loan problems.[11]

The Wall Street Journal points out that although loss deferral is helping to finance the increased borrowing that has been propelling the economy, 'it can't push all the bad news into the future'. Ultimately, Americans may be forced to recognize that the patchwork which has kept short-term economic indicators purring has caused long-term problems of alarming magnitude. With that revelation is also likely to come the recognition that in deferring the solution of many economic problems like bad debts, our capacity to respond resolutely on so many fronts is seriously impaired.

SOCIAL DARWINISM

Reaganomics is none other than the resurgence of *laissez-faire*. It became particularly attractive in the early 1980s because of the excesses of the 1970s. Stagflation produced a malaise in the American spirit. Reaganomics offered an alternative to the failed Keynesian policies of the post-Vietnam War era. And it offered Americans a renewed confidence that prosperity for the middle classes could be won again by redevotion to frontier values of hard work and independence. The appeal to get the government off of the people's backs touched Americans as deeply and as basically as nineteenth-century Americans were touched by the values of Jacksonian democracy. The crucial difference, however, is that Ronald Reagan is out of touch with the reality of his time.

Reaganomics constitutes the rebirth of a kind of Social Darwinism which champions the survival of the fittest. The economically weak are alleged to survive only because of the skills, the industry and the risk-taking of the strong. Getting the government off people's backs implies the unfettering of the strong to pursue their self-interests. Only in doing so could the wealthy – and the poor, also – be well served. Domestic programmes in the administrations of Kennedy and Johnson had redistributed income and power away from the economically strong. But if the weak are to be cared for in the *laissez-faire* society of the 1980s, that care must be in the form of voluntary charity rather than in the form of entitlements. Entitlements to the poor weaken the strong. Unless the fetters of government are removed, so the argument goes, the strong will be dragged down by the weak, and ultimately they will neither provide proper sustenance for themselves nor for the weak.

The *laissez-faire* resurgence found support among conservative and free market economists who provided rationale – even 'proofs' – for government deregulation and disengagement. Among the compelling arguments of science are the elegant proofs that economic welfare is maximized in market economies when pure competition prevails. The logic of deregulation appealed to the American psyche long before the election of Ronald Reagan. In 1979, the mentality led to the takeover by conservative monetarists of the Federal Reserve, long a bastion of Keynesian views, fully a year before Reagan's election.

But in the headlong rush towards the reimplementation of the competitive philosophy, politicians and economists failed to acknowledge that the dicta from which their neoclassical prescriptions are drawn is based upon a stationary vision of the world. Since profit is zero in such a world, the class of capitalists is reduced to function as a class of rentiers. The only justification for the private retention of capital assets in such a stationary society is the argument for retaining the status quo.

WHY REAGANOMICS FAILED

The *laissez-faire* resurgence was predestined to failure for reasons similar to the failure of Keynesian economics in the 1970s. Both doctrines are based upon metaphysical views of the world which have their origins in eighteenth-century natural law. The problem with using an economic system based on natural law is that the theory that is derived from it fails to account for differences between extant society and the archetypal ideal. To the extent that extant society is in conformance with the assumptions upon which ideal society is thought to be based, then a natural law-based theory will be both explanatory and predictive. But if actual society diverges from ideal society, then the theory will provide dicta which lead to societal suboptimization. Such is the case with the contemporary *laissez-faire* resurgence. Its prescriptions are couched in an ideological view that the pursuit of self-interest always benefits the commonweal.

The practical logic of attaining such a blissful outcome is mitigated by the complexity of the world around us. Fewer rules and less structure in the selection of investments, today, can weaken the economic status of groups within society, as well as provoking economic stagnation. Those whose lots improve through the reimposition of *laissez-faire* values become the champions of its dogma. They are its ideologues – its impractical idealists – for they defend it in spite of its inability to deliver *overall* positive outcomes, so long as it delivers positive outcomes for *them*.

RONALD REAGAN – IDEOLOGUE

Reaganomics has failed because it is a 'rearguard' action to rescue a failing vision of who we are, of what we have been, and of what we may become. Its desire for an improvement in 'the wealth of nations' is legitimate. But that goal has been pursued dogmatically, perhaps because legitimate alternatives have already been rejected, have been unavailable, or have been hidden from view. With each new revelation of economic failure, the ideologues have redoubled their efforts to prove that their prescription is the right one, if only we persist in trying to make it work.

Ronald Reagan is portrayed – and portrays himself – as anti-intellectual. It is the thinkers, accordingly, 'who foul things up'. And it is men of bravery and dedication to time-honoured frontier values that succeed when they are unshackled from government restriction. The ruse of Ronald Reagan is that he is not anti-intellectual, but pseudo-intellectual. He is the champion of a doctrine with a carefully reasoned intellectual component. He is the 'stalking horse' and defender, intellectual and otherwise, of the *laissez-faire* resurgence.

We have described *laissez-faire* as counter-intuitive to the logic of the commons. It asserts that if individuals act in their own self-interest – if they throw their garbage on the commons, so to speak – then everyone will actually benefit. We have revealed the inappropriateness of this counter-intuitive claim in the workings (and non-workings) of contemporary capitalist economies.

As the principal ideologue of *laissez-faire*, we may describe Ronald Reagan as someone who holds tenaciously to the doctrine, regardless of the outcome; but his position demands much more than mere ideological leadership. He is President of the United States and accountable for the welfare of all of its people. Many of America's most vulnerable citizens are being harmed severely by the policies of his administration. It grows increasingly difficult for the young to succeed, yet the plight of an entire generation is casually dismissed with aphorisms and anecdotes about the values of hard work and personal sacrifice. The style is cavalier, for it dismisses legitimate human hardship as the fault of the individual, rather than the responsibility of the social and economic system. As the champion of the failed *laissez-faire* resurgence, Ronald Reagan is an ideologue who has thrown his intellectual garbage upon the American commons.

12 Recommendations

Once again *laissez-faire* has come to crisis. It no longer works appropriately because the world has changed since the eighteenth century, which then was more compatible with Adam Smith's vision of natural law. Most aspects of capitalism still work, or can be made to work. These include the private ownership of capital, and the institution of the unregulated (or partially regulated) market for the allocation of current output and resources. But the aspect of doctrinaire capitalism which has become inoperative, specifically, is the ability of market economies to make choices affecting the future. Now the allocation of output and resources for the future must be governed through non-market collective choice.

Doctrinaire capitalism was first revealed as a failure during the Great Depression. The decade of the 1930s was a period of protracted disequilibrium in which current saving substantially exceeded current investment. Say's Law asserts that saving and investment equality will be realized instantaneously and continuously. Keynes rejected Say's Law and introduced a theoretical solution for the repair of capitalism, called mixed capitalism. It continued to embody the concept of the free market for both present and future choices. But unlike pure *laissez-faire*, in Keynes's 'mixed' system it became the legitimate function of government to create purchasing power to overcome any imbalance between saving and investment. It is accomplished through a government-generated demand stimulus sufficient to obtain and to maintain full employment. This treatise appends Keynes's demand-stimulating dicta and argues that stabilization policies should also be accompanied by disincentives to hoard, either in the form of taxes or direct regulation.

Gold was the principle object of hoarders during the Great Depression. Hoarding behaviour was dissuaded, at least in part, by making illegal the holding of gold by American citizens. More recently, during the inflationary 1970s, real estate and other inelastically supplied assets have been hoarded speculatively or as a protection against monetary depreciation. But recent forms of hoarding have not been taxed or regulated. Hoarding subverts capital formation. As an alternative to monetary austerity, which was used to curtail inflation early in this decade, the inflation problem may be resolved

179

by imposing a special tax on income received from trading real estate and other fixed assets.

In the early 1980s the hoarding problem was structurally similar to the 1970s, but it revealed itself uniquely. Transactors were lured from holding capital and even from trading in real estate and the like, to trading in high yield, interest-bearing finance. Financial hoarding may also be mitigated by imposing a higher differential tax on income received from trading in interest-bearing finance.

More recently – in the mid-1980s – many transactors are liquidating finance to acquire equity holdings in common stock. Although there is some danger that the stock market may become overbid, the most significant and lasting economic danger occurs when the sale of equity is used for non-productive purposes such as the financing of corporate raids. Such forms of hoarding may be mitigated by imposing what Keynes called a transfer tax on the non-productive sale of assets. Regulation of corporate acquisitions may also be utilized to countermand the finance-leeching of capital by corporations.

Setting a higher differential tax on income received from the inflated sale prices of assets held in fixed supply, from interest-bearing finance, or'from corporate raids, is a means of repairing the second glitch of economic theory, which is the profit lacuna. A differential income tax is a means of specifying what the rate of profit should be. The process which leads to such a differential income tax structure is a form of non-market collective choice known as indicative economic planning.

Before the rate of profit on capital can be specified by establishing tax disincentives for hoarding, the nature of capital must first be determined. In a dynamic society, capital is the agent of change necessary to shift from the status quo composition and quantity of output, to some future output quantity and composition. In the contemporary milieu decisions affecting capital holding are inevitably nationalistic in their perspective. Because of this, there lurks an ever present danger that indicative economic planning may serve as the pretext for a dangerous rise of jingoism. The economic realities which give rise to indicative economic planning are also likely to elicit the most profound reshaping of international relations since the Second World War.

NATIONAL LEADERSHIP

It is at the national level – rather than at local, regional or international levels – that stabilization policies can be made coherent. It is here that a society has the power to create money, to regulate trade with other societies, and to levy substantial taxes. It is the United States Congress that should act to regulate hoarding, and to tax income received from non-productive sources at a higher differential rate. To do so, national governments including the United States must determine what constitutes productive investment, and therefore what does not. Such determinations must be preceded by 'scenario building' about what the set of possible and attractive choices might be. Scenario selection ultimately leads to conclusions regarding what constitutes productive capital necessary to attain that scenario.

In the United States an organization such as the Congressional Budget Office (CBO) could assume leadership for necessary scenario building implicit in economic planning. It would evaluate alternate scenarios for the future, consider any implications for implementing each scenario, and also consider any ramifications for various special interest groups likely to be affected.

Ultimately the gargantuan responsibility of passing legislation which impinges upon a plethora of special interest groups must fall due. Given the proclivity of Congress to dodge the 'hard choices', the success of the process is likely to leave many observers of American politics less than sanguine. Choices would be required about what future outcomes should be, the quantity and mix of productive resources necessary to attain them, and those classes of income recipients that would be taxed at a differentially higher rate. Indicative economic planning would also require comprehensive and articulated decisions on international tariff and trade relationships. Among these would be policies regulating not only the importation of foreign products, but the possible subsidization of some American exports, and the domestic control of international financial movements by multinational corporations and private individuals. Otherwise, without the assertion of national economic priorities, the finance-leeching of domestic capital will continue unabated, or it will intensify.

CONVENTIONAL WISDOM, 1986

During the second half of 1986 a growing concern is being expressed that a recession may overtake the American economy in 1987, although the mainstream of the conventional wisdom continues to predict economic expansion. Real growth during the first half of 1986 was scarcely 1 per cent. The conventional wisdom holds that deficit reduction is crucial to economic health. It is argued that buoyant growth – in the range of 3 to 4 per cent – can be obtained throughout the balance of the decade if federal dissaving is curtailed. The Gramm–Rudman law proposes to slash federal budget deficits from the $200 billion range, to zero, over a five-year period ending in 1991.

The crucial question for stabilization policy pertains to the possible effects of deficit reduction on economic health, if a recession is revealed to be imminent. Certainly deficit reduction during a period of expansion is compatible with Keynes's dicta. It is likely to reduce competition for loanable funds, which in turn should lower interest rates, and ultimately stimulate capital accumulation and growth. But the reduction of government spending during a period of sluggish growth is likely to exacerbate recession greatly. Americans may ultimately be required to face the political reality that the only time budget reduction is warranted is in the early part of a recovery.

Monetary growth has far outpaced the growth of real GNP in both 1985 and 1986. Even though inflation in the United States has been held in check during the Reagan years, an eventual return to inflation, resulting from the current money build up, is a rational expectation. If so, the United States is likely again to experience the pressures of the 1970s repeated in the late 1980s. Renewed inflation could lead to transactor hedging in real estate and other assets held in fixed supply. Eventually, as the monetary authority attempts again to reign in inflation by tightening the money supply, interest rates are likely to be driven dramatically higher. And savvy transactors are then likely to shift from holding non-productive real estate to holding non-productive finance. Later in this pernicious cycle, common stocks may again become comparatively attractive.

OTHER RECOMMENDATIONS

Some other recommendations that are also generated from the application of disequilibrium analysis to contemporary economic dysfunction are as follows:

1. The 'reregulation' of some key industries, such as telecommunications, should be reconsidered. The conventional wisdom of the 1970s was that breaking up the American Telephone and Telegraph (AT&T) monopoly would promote competition, stimulate efficient resource allocation within the industry, and therefore engender econ-

omic growth. On the contrary, however, deregulation may have disturbed the attainment and retention of the Marshallian short period by encouraging producers to seek higher rates of return outside the immediate industry. AT&T, for instance, has unsuccessfully launched a line of personal computers. Such ventures constitute disinvestment, from the original perspective of the public interest. The attainment of buoyant rates of domestic or export growth may require a higher rate of return on the assets of telecommunications and other key industries than unregulated markets can provide.

2. An increase in public investment projects should be considered. The conventional wisdom holds that major capital formulation should occur in private markets. But public projects such as the GI Bill, the interstate highway system and NASA have been among America's most vital growth stimulants. In some cases, the sheer size of the activity makes it a candidate for being launched in the public sector. In others, the activity may be a pure public good for which development is uniquely suited to the public sector.

However, in spite of the unique capacity of government to undertake social investment, a caveat is certainly in order. Some public investment projects have been engaged very effectively by government, whereas others have become major débâcles. Examples of the failures of the past decade, during which energy policy figured prominently, are the now abandoned synthetic fuels programme to create petroleum products from coal, tar sands and shale, and the Washington State Public Power Supply System (WPPSS) nuclear power plant débâcle which resulted in the largest single default on public bonds in the nation's history.

3. Recent history suggests a substantial correlation between increases in the stock of fiat money and the decline in the rate of growth. The feasibility of reinstituting a commodity-backed money system, in whole or in part, may be appropriate. A multicommodity system might prove feasible, and could be backed by homogeneous industrial commodities (e.g. crude oil, sulphuric acid) and surplus commodities such as agricultural products. Generally there is no need to limit, or even to require, the inclusion of precious metals in such a system.

4. The United States has only limited experience in generating revenues through the application of consumption taxes. Even so, these taxes should probably be used more extensively. Among the advantages of consumption taxes are that they can act as demand

suppressants during periods in which more saving and less consumption may be indicated. Also, since classes of goods and services can be taxed at differential rates, consumption taxes provide a means for discouraging certain forms of consumption which may have distributional implications (such as luxury goods). These may also discourage certain import industries (e.g. video tape recorders) for which contraction, rather than expansion, may be indicated.

A FINAL CAVEAT

With the 1988 presidential election approaching, political pressures for an economic 'quick fix' will mount. But simplistic solutions are usually not germaine to complex, intractable problems. This is particularly true with regard to contemporary economic dysfunction. The 'good old days' of the 1950s and 1960s are probably gone forever. Prospects for improving the standard of living at an average compound rate in the vicinity of 3 per cent per year are quite unrealistic, at least in the foreseeable future. Pundits and politicians always make compelling election year arguments and promises. Hopefully those promises will be weighed by an increasingly sophisticated electorate that responds to promises of 'pie in the sky' with abhorrence.

Indicative economic planning is an idea which is coming of age, not because of its optimistic vision of the future but because of pragmatic necessity. Economic survival mandates that we face up to the irrevocable changes that are occurring in the compressed world in which we live, work, and hopefully coexist. The eminent and immediate goal of capitalist society should not be to thrive in ways previously unattained, but to survive with as much dignity and with as many of the appropriate vestiges of the established order as can be defended and can be mustered.

Notes and References

2 Isaac Newton and Economics

1. Eighteenth-century political economy was an admixture of natural law and moral philosophy applied to production and trade. It was highly metaphysical in character. In the *Theory of Moral Sentiments* (1759), for instance, Adam Smith attempted to identify the origins of moral approval and disapproval. Smith argued that, even though man is a creature of self-interest, moral judgements can be made on the basis of other human considerations, through what he called the faculty of sympathy. This works, according to Smith, by holding self-interest in abeyance and putting oneself in the position of an impartial observer, who reaches a sympathetic judgement about the approval or disapproval of a particular human behaviour, apart from the conventional criteria of self-interest.

   In the *Wealth of Nations* (1776), however, Smith appears to take somewhat of a less egalitarian view of self-interested action. On page 14 he writes:

   > But man has almost constant occasion for the help of his brethren, and it is vain to expect it from their benevolence only . . . It is not from the benevolence of the butcher, the brewer, or the baker, that we expect our dinner, but from their regard to their own interest.

   To Smith, moral behaviour, could be isolated, objectified, and therefore made to be self-evident. The difficulty with Smith's method, of course, is that different individuals, when placed in the same situation of choice, may come to divergent conclusions about the rightness or wrongness of a particular human action. This occurs not only because of differences in individual willingness and ability to become detached from self-interest, but more particularly, because of vast differences that exist among individuals with regard to values and beliefs.

2. The novice reader may be interested to pursue an extension of the demand and supply apparatus, to long-run equilibrium, by consulting a principles-level economics text.

3. Certainly Say presented the contention as much more than a condition for the occurrence of systemic equilibrium that will in governance by natural law be harmoniously and instantaneously realized. The footnote by Say in 'Of the Vent of Demand for Products' from *A Treatise on Political Economy*, C.R. Prinsep, translator (Boston, 1824) indicates that he raised the possibility of produce being brought to market with the intention of hoarding the proceeds of sale. Certainly the foundations of classical and neoclassical economy are replete with market illustrations of 'tâtonnement', or groping towards equilibrium.

3 A Disequilibrium View

1. The standard usage is that realized or *ex post* saving is identically equal to realized or *ex post* investment, either as accumulated over a period of time or as rates experienced in an instant of time, regardless of any equilibrium conditions. If at any level of output, desired or *ex ante* investment is less than intended or *ex ante* saving, then the result will be some failure of expectations to be realized. Since equality between saving and investment can occur in the conventional model simultaneous with involuntary unemployment, the equilibrium condition need not be applied in that model. Rather, it becomes introduced as a matter of practical convention in application to the analysis of extant economies.

4 Why Keynesian Stabilization Policy Doesn't Work?

1. Tabular and graphical examples of Keynesian analysis are drawn from Campbell R. McConnell (1984) *Economics*.
2. The perfectly horizontal investment curve used for the convenience of exposition in this illustration assumes that the investment plans of business are independent of the current level of income. In reality the investment schedule may be slightly upsloping, suggesting some degree of interest and income elasticity.

5 Unexplained Problems

1. See Mark Drabenstott (1985).

6 Asset Conservation

1. The careful reader without an economic background may be acutely aware that a 'leap' has been made for pedagogical purposes. In order to follow the argument more carefully, consult a college level economic principles text, with particular attention to chapters on production, cost, and demand for variable inputs.

8 Zero Sum Society

1. Haruki Kamiya, Executive Vice President of Nippon Steel, quoted in a syndicated article by Sam Jameson of the *Los Angeles Times*, carried in the *Seattle Times*, 25 June 1984.

10 The Disintegration of the World Economy

1. Albers Business Forum, Seattle University, 12 April 1985.
2. *The Wall Street Journal*, 9 August 1985.

Notes and References 187

3. *Seattle Times*, 6 March 1986.
4. *The Wall Street Journal*, 27 January 1986.

11 Reaganomics

1. See William Greider (1982) and David Stockman (1986).
2. See Irwin L. Kellner (1984) January.
3. See George A. Kahn (1985).
4. See Irwin L. Kellner (1984) September.
5. See Marilyn Moon and Isabel V. Sawhill (1984).
6. *Seattle Times*, 25 July 1986.
7. *Seattle Times*, 2 February 1986.
8. *Seattle Times*, 29 July 1986.
9. *Newsweek*, 10 March 1986.
10. *Newsweek*, 10 February 1986.
11. *The Wall Street Journal*, 8 January 1986.

Bibliography

ASCHHEIM, JOSEPH and CHING-YAO HSIEH (1969) *Macroeconomics: Income and Monetary Theory*, Merrill.

BARDACH, EUGENE (1984) 'Implementing Industrial Policy', in *The Industrial Policy Debate* ed. Chalmers Johnson, ICS Press.

BERG, N.A. (1981) 'Resources Conservation Act: New Window on the Future' in *Economics, Ethics, Ecology*, ed. W.E. Jeske, Ankeny, Iowa, Conservation Society of America.

BERLE, A.A. and G.C. MEANS (1932) *The Modern Corporation and Private Property*, Macmillan.

BOSWORTH, BARRY P. (1984) 'Capital Formation, Technology and Economic Policy', in *Industrial Change and Public Policy Symposium*, Federal Reserve Bank of Kansas City.

CLARK, JOHN BATES (1899) *The Distribution of Wealth*, Macmillan.

CLOWER, ROBERT (1974) 'Reflections on Science . . . and Economics', *Intermountain Economic Review*, 5.

COOPER, RICHARD N. (1984) 'Linkage Effects', in *The Global Repercussions of US Monetary and Fiscal Policy* ed. Kaufman, Hewlett and Kenen, ch. 3, Ballinger.

DAVID, P.A. (1975) *Technical Choice, Innovation and Economic Growth*, Cambridge University Press.

DRABENSTOTT, MARK (1985) 'US Agriculture: The Difficult Adjustment Continues', *Economic Review of the Federal Reserve Bank of Kansas City*, December.

ECONOMIC REPORT OF THE PRESIDENT (1987) Washington, D.C., Government Printing Office.

EKELUND, ROBERT B., Jr and ROBERT F. HEBERT (1983) *History of Economic Theory and Method*, McGraw-Hill.

GREIDER, WILLIAM (1982) *The Education of David Stockman and Other Americans*, E.P. Dutton.

HENDERSON, YOLANDA KODRZYCKI (1984) 'Tax Reform: An Item For Any Industrial Policy Agenda', in *The Industrial Policy Debate* ed. Chalmers Johnson, ICS Press.

HOADLEY, WALTER E. (1984) 'Banking and Finance: The Cost of Capital in Japan and the United States', in *The Industrial Policy Debate* ed. Chalmers Johnson, ICS Press.

JENNY, HANS (1984) 'The Making and Unmaking of a Fertile Soil', in *Meeting the Expectations of the Land* eds Wes Jackson, Wendell Berry, Bruce Colman, North Point Press.

KAHN, GEORGE A. (1985) 'Investment in Recession and Recovery', *Economic Review of the Federal Reserve Bank of Kansas City*, November.

KELLNER, IRWIN L. (1984) *Manufacturers Hanover Economic Report*, January.

KELLNER, IRWIN L. (1984) *Manufacturers Hanover Economic Report*, September.

189

KELLNER, IRWIN L. (1987) *Manufacturers Hanover Economic Report*, January.
KEYNES, JOHN MAYNARD (1936) *The General Theory of Employment, Interest and Money*, Harcourt, Brace & World.
KRAUSS, MELVYN (1984) '"Europeanizing" the US Economy: The Enduring Appeal of the Corporate State', in *The Industrial Policy Debate* ed. Chalmers Johnson, ICS Press.
LEIJONHUFVUD, AXEL (1968) *On Keynesian Economics and the Economics of Keynes*, Oxford.
LEVY, FRANK S. and RICHARD C. MICHEL (1985) *The Economic Future of the Baby Boom*, Urban Institute, Revised, December 5.
LUNDBERG, E. (1961) *Produktivitet och Rantabilitet*, Norstedt & Soner.
MCCONNELL, CAMPBELL R. (1984) *Economics*, 9th edn, McGraw-Hill.
MCCRAW, THOMAS K. (1984) 'Business and Government: The Origins of the Adversary Relationship', *California Management Review*, XXVI, Winter 1984.
MOON, MARYILYN and ISABEL V. SAWHILL (1984) 'Family Incomes', in *The Reagan Record* eds Palmer and Sawhill, Balinger.
OLSON, MANCUR (1982) *The Rise and Decline of Nations*, Yale University Press.
OZAKI, ROBERT S. (1984) 'How Japanese Industrial Policy Works', in *The Industrial Policy Debate* ed. Chalmers Johnson, ICS Press.
POPPER, KARL R. (1962) *Logic of Scientific Discovery*, Basic Books.
RIMA, INGRID HAHNE (1978) *Development of Economic Analysis*, Irwin.
ROBINSON, JOAN (1964) *Economic Philosophy*, Doubleday-Anchor.
ROBINSON, JOAN (1971) *Economic Heresies*, Basic Books.
ROSE, STEVE (1985) *Social Stratification in the US*, Pantheon.
SAHAL, DEVENDRA (1981) *Patterns of Technological Innovation*, Addison-Wesley.
SAINT-ETIENNE, CHRISTIAN (1984) *The Great Depression*, Hoover Institution.
SHACKLE, G.L.S. (1958) *Time in Economics*, North Holland.
STOCKMAN, DAVID (1986) *The Triumph of Politics*, Harper & Row.
STRANGE, MARTY (1984) 'The Economic Structure of a Sustainable Agriculture', in *Meeting the Expectations of the Land* eds Wes Jackson, Wendell Berry, Bruce Colman, North Point Press.
SUMMERS, LAWRENCE H. (1984) 'Commentary on Changes in US Industrial Structure', in *Industrial Change and Public Policy*, Federal Reserve Bank of Kansas City.
THUROW, LESTER C. (1985) *The Zero-Sum Solution*, Simon & Schuster.
WASHINGTON STATE LEGISLATURE, *House Ways and Means Committee Report*, 4 October 1985.
WICKSTEED, E.H. (1894) *An Essay on the Co-ordination of the Laws of Distribution*, Macmillan. Reprinted in the Scarce Tracts series by London School of Economics.
WILDAVSKY, AARON (1984) 'Squaring the Political Circle', in *Industrial Policy Debate* ed. Chalmers Johnson, ICS Press.

Index